ABORTION: LEGISLATIVE AND LEGAL ISSUES

D1207279

LAWS AND LEGISLATION SERIES

LAWS AND LEGISLATION SERIES

ABORTION: LEGISLATIVE AND LEGAL ISSUES

KEVIN G. NOLAN
EDITOR

Nova Science Publishers, Inc.
New York

For permission to use material from this book please contact us:
Telephone 631-231-7269; Fax 631-231-8175
Web Site: http://www.novapublishers.com

NOTICE TO THE READER

LIBRARY OF CONGRESS CATALOGING-IN-PUBLICATION DATA

Abortion : legislative and legal issues / editors, Kevin G. Nolan.
    p. cm.
  Includes bibliographical references and index.
  ISBN 978-1-60741-522-0 (hardcover : alk. paper)
  1. Abortion--Law and legislation--United States. I. Nolan, Kevin G.
  KF3771.A25 2009
  342.7308'4--dc22
                                2009032006

Published by Nova Science Publishers, Inc. ✦ *New York*

CONTENTS

PREFACE

In Roe v. Wade, the U.S. Supreme Court determined that the Constitution protects a woman's decision whether or not to terminate her pregnancy. In a companion case, Doe v. Bolton, the Court held further that a state may not unduly burden a woman's fundamental right to abortion by prohibiting or substantially limiting access to the means of effectuating her decision. Instead of settling the issue, the Court's decisions kindled heated debate and precipitated a variety of governmental actions at the national, state and local levels designed either to nullify the rulings or hinder their effectuation. These governmental regulations have, in turn, spawned further litigation in which resulting judicial refinements in the law have been no more successful in dampening the controversy. This book offers an overview of the development of abortion law from 1973 to the present. Beginning with a brief discussion of the historical background, the book analyzes the leading Supreme Court decisions over the past 34 years, emphasizing particularly the landmark decisions of Roe v. Wade and others. This book consists of public documents which have been located, gathered, combined, reformatted, and enhanced with a subject index, selectively edited and bound to provide easy access.

Chapter 1 - In *Roe v. Wade*, 410 U.S. 113 (1973), the U.S. Supreme Court determined that the Constitution protects a woman's decision whether or not to terminate her pregnancy. In a companion case, *Doe v. Bolton*, 410 U.S. 179 (1973), the Court held further that a state may not unduly burden a woman's fundamental right to abortion by prohibiting or substantially limiting access to the means of effectuating her decision. Rather than settle the issue, the Court's decisions kindled heated debate and precipitated a variety of governmental actions at the national, state and local levels designed either to nullify the rulings or hinder their effectuation. These governmental regulations have, in turn, spawned further litigation in which resulting judicial refinements in the law have been no more successful in dampening the controversy.

The law with respect to abortion in mid-19th century America followed the common law of England in all but a few states. By the time of the Civil War, a number of states had begun to revise their statutes in order to prohibit abortion at all stages of gestation, with various exceptions for therapeutic abortions. The year 1967 marked the first victory of an abortion reform movement with the passage of liberalizing legislation in Colorado. The legislation was based on the Model Penal Code. Between 1967 and 1973, approximately one-third of the states had adopted, either in whole or in part, the Model Penal Code's provisions allowing abortion in instances other than where only the mother's life was in danger. Between 1968 and 1972, abortion statutes of many states were challenged on the grounds of vagueness, violation of the fundamental right of privacy, and denial of equal protection. In 1973, the Court ruled in *Roe* and *Doe* that Texas and Georgia statutes regulating abortion interfered to an unconstitutional extent with a woman's right to decide whether to terminate her pregnancy. The decisions rested upon the conclusion that the Fourteenth Amendment right of personal privacy encompassed a woman's decision whether to carry a pregnancy to term.

The Supreme Court's decisions in *Roe* and *Doe* did not address a number of important abortionrelated issues which have been raised subsequently by state actions seeking to restrict the scope of the Court's rulings. These include the issues of informed consent, spousal consent, parental consent, and reporting requirements. In addition, *Roe* and *Doe* never resolved the question of what, if any, type of abortion procedures may be required or prohibited by statute. In 1989, the Court indicated in *Webster v. Reproductive Health Services*, 492 U.S. 490, that, while it was not overruling *Roe* and *Doe*, it was willing to apply a less stringent standard of review to state restrictions respecting a woman's right to an abortion. Then, in 1992, in *Planned Parenthood of Southeastern Pennsylvania v. Casey*, 505 U.S. 833 (1992), the Court rejected specifically *Roe*'s strict scrutiny standard and adopted the undue burden analysis. In 2000, in *Stenberg v. Carhart*, 530 U.S. 914 (2000), the Court determined that a Nebraska statute prohibiting the performance of "partial-birth" abortions was unconstitutional. In 2007, however, the Court upheld the federal Partial-Birth Abortion Ban Act of 2003 in *Gonzales v. Carhart*, 550 U.S. 124 (2007). In upholding the federal act, the Court distinguished between the federal measure and the Nebraska statute.

Chapter 2 - In 1973, the U.S. Supreme Court concluded in *Roe v. Wade* that the U.S. Constitution protects a woman's decision to terminate her pregnancy. In *Doe v. Bolton*, a companion decision, the Court found that a state may not unduly burden the exercise of that fundamental right with regulations that prohibit or substantially limit access to the means of effectuating the decision to have an abortion. Rather than settle the issue, the Court's rulings since *Roe* and *Doe* have continued to generate debate and have precipitated a variety of governmental actions at the national, state, and local levels designed either to nullify the rulings or limit their effect. These governmental regulations have, in turn, spawned further litigation in which resulting judicial refinements in the law have been no more successful in dampening the controversy.

In recent years, the rights enumerated in *Roe* have been redefined by decisions such as *Webster v. Reproductive Health Services*, which gave greater leeway to the States to restrict abortion, and *Rust v. Sullivan*, which narrowed the scope of permissible abortion-related activities that are linked to federal funding. The Court's decision in *Planned Parenthood of Southeastern Pennsylvania v. Casey*, which established the "undue burden" standard for determining whether abortion restrictions are permissible, gave Congress additional impetus to move on statutory responses to the abortion issue, such as the Freedom of Choice Act.

In each Congress since 1973, constitutional amendments to prohibit abortion have been introduced. These measures have been considered in committee, but none has been passed by either the House or the Senate.

Legislation to prohibit a specific abortion procedure, the so-called "partial-birth" abortion procedure, was passed in the 108th Congress. The Partial-Birth Abortion Ban Act appears to be one of the only examples of Congress restricting the performance of a medical procedure. Legislation that would prohibit the knowing transport of a minor across state lines for the purpose of obtaining an abortion has been introduced in numerous Congresses.

Since *Roe*, Congress has attached abortion funding restrictions to various appropriations measures. The greatest focus has been on restricting Medicaid abortions under the annual appropriations for the Department of Health and Human Services. This series of restrictions is popularly known as the "Hyde Amendments." Restrictions on the use of appropriated funds affect numerous federal entities, including the Department of Justice, where federal funds may not be used to perform abortions in the federal prison system except in cases of rape or endangerment of the mother. Such restrictions also have an impact in the District of Columbia, where both federal and local funds may not be used to perform abortions except in cases of rape, incest or where the mother is endangered, and affect international organizations like the United Nations Population Fund, which receives funds through the annual Foreign Operations appropriations measure.

Chapter 3 - In 1993, President Clinton modified the military policy on providing abortions at military medical facilities. Under the change directed by the President, military medical facilities were allowed to perform abortions if paid for entirely with non-Department of Defense (DOD) funds (i.e., privately funded). Although arguably consistent with statutory language barring the use of Defense Department funds, the President's policy overturned a former interpretation of existing law barring the availability of these services. On December 1, 1995, H.R. 2126, the FY1996 DOD appropriations act, became law (P.L. 104-61). Included in this law was language barring the use of funds to administer any policy that permits the performance of abortions at any DOD facility except where the life of the mother would be endangered if the fetus were carried to term or where the pregnancy resulted from an act of rape or incest. Language was also included in the FY1996 DOD Authorization Act (P.L. 104-106, February 10, 1996) prohibiting the use of DOD facilities in the performance of abortions. These served to reverse the President's 1993 policy change. Recent attempts to change or modify these laws have failed.

Over the last three decades, the availability of abortion services at military medical facilities has been subjected to numerous changes and interpretations. Within the last 15 years, Congress has considered numerous amendments to effectuate such changes. Although Congress, in 1992, passed one such amendment to make abortions available at overseas installation, it was vetoed.

The changes ordered by the President did not necessarily have the effect of greatly increasing access to abortion services. Abortions are generally not performed at military medical facilities in the continental United States. In addition, few have been performed at these facilities abroad for a number of reasons. First, the U.S. military follows the prevailing laws and rules of foreign countries regarding abortion. Second, the military has had a difficult time finding health care professionals in uniform willing to perform the procedure.

With the enactment of P.L. 104-61 and P.L. 104-106, these questions became moot, because now, neither DOD funds nor facilities may be used to administer any policy that provides for abortions at any DOD facility, except where the life of the mother may be endangered if the fetus were carried to term. Privately-funded abortions at military facilities are permitted when the pregnancy was the result of an act of rape or incest.

There has been little legislative activity affecting the military on this issue. The last major effort occurred with an amendment to the House version of the FY2007 National Defense Authorization Act would allow DOD facilities outside the U.S. to perform privately-funded abortions. This language was rejected by the conference committee.

Chapter 4 - On August 24, 2006, the Food and Drug Administration (FDA) announced the approval of an application to switch Plan B, an emergency contraceptive, from a prescription-only drug to an over-the-counter (OTC) drug for women 18 years of age and older. Plan B will only be sold in pharmacies or healthcare clinics. It will continue to be dispensed as a prescription drug for women 17 years old and younger. Plan B is a brand of post-coital contraceptive that is administered within a few hours or days of unprotected intercourse. Emergency contraception prevents pregnancy; it does not disrupt an established pregnancy.

Approval of the switch to OTC status for Plan B has been controversial. Some Members of Congress urged the FDA to deny OTC status for Plan B. Individuals who criticize the three-year delay in deciding to switch to OTC believe that Bush Administration policy and FDA actions were based on political and ideological considerations rather than on sound science. Conservative religious and pro-life groups believe Plan B may increase unsafe sexual activity and should be used only under the supervision of a healthcare professional and, therefore, should not be available OTC. Their major concern with Plan B, however, is that it might prevent the implantation of an embryo in the uterus, which to pro-life groups constitutes abortion. However, the medical community does not consider prevention of implantation to be an abortion, and FDA does not classify Plan B as an abortion drug.

Emergency contraceptives are currently available without a prescription in more than 40 countries. According to Barr Pharmaceuticals, sales of Plan B in the United States have doubled since August 2006, "rising from about $40 million a year to what will probably be close to $80 million for 2007." Women's health advocates claim that OTC status will improve access to the drug, thereby reducing the number of unintended pregnancies and reducing the number of abortions. However, a medical literature review, published in April 2007, found that "advance provision of emergency contraception did not reduce pregnancy rates when compared to conventional provision.... The interventions tested thus far have not reduced overall pregnancy rates in the populations studied."

The Office of Violence Against Women within the Department of Justice (DOJ) has developed guidelines for the treatment of sexual assault victims. The guidelines, released in September 2004, have been criticized by numerous organizations because they do not mention offering emergency contraception to female rape victims. In January 2005, a letter signed by 97 Members of Congress was sent to the Director of the Office on Violence Against Women expressing concern over the failure to mention emergency contraception and urging that the guidelines be changed to include such information.

Legislation introduced in the 110th Congress (S. 21/H.R. 819, H.R. 464, S. 1240, H.R. 2064/S. 1800, H.R. 2503, H.R. 2596/S. 1555) aims to ensure that Plan

B is made available to women in general and sexual assault victims in particular or encourage education and provide information about Plan B.

Chapter 5 - Conscience clause laws allow medical providers to refuse to provide services to which they have religious or moral objections. In some cases, these laws are designed to excuse such providers from performing abortions. While substantive conscience clause legislation has not been approved, appropriations bills that include conscience clause provisions have been passed. This chapter describes the history of conscience clauses as they relate to abortion law and provides a legal analysis of the effects of such laws. The report also reviews recent proposed regulations to implement some of the conscience clause laws.

Conscience clause laws allow medical providers to refuse to provide services to which they have religious or moral objections. These laws are generally designed to reconcile "the conflict between religious health care providers who provide care in accordance with their religious beliefs and the patients who want access to medical care that these religious providers find objectionable."[1] Although conscience clause laws have grown to encompass protections for entities that object to a wide array of medical services and procedures, such as providing contraceptives or terminating life-support, the original focus of conscience clause laws was on permitting health care providers to refuse to participate in abortion or sterilization procedures on religious or moral grounds.

Chapter 6 - The Partial-Birth Abortion Ban Act ("PBABA" or "the act") was signed into law on November 5, 2003. Within two days of its enactment, the PBABA was enjoined by federal district courts in Nebraska, California, and New York. Since that time, the U.S. Courts of Appeals for the Second, Eighth, and Ninth Circuits have affirmed lower court decisions that have found the act unconstitutional.

This chapter examines *Gonzales v. Carhart* and *Gonzales v. Planned Parenthood*, the partial-birth abortion decisions from the Eighth and Ninth Circuits. In spring 2006, the U.S. Supreme Court agreed to review the two decisions. This chapter provides background information on the PBABA and explores the arguments put forth by the parties.

The Partial-Birth Abortion Ban Act ("PBABA" or "the act") was signed into law on November 5, 2003.[1] Within two days of its enactment, the PBABA was enjoined by federal district courts in Nebraska, California, and New York.[2] Since that time, the U.S. Courts of Appeals for the Second, Eighth, and Ninth Circuits have affirmed lower court decisions that have found the act unconstitutional.[3]

In spring 2006, the U.S. Supreme Court agreed to review *Gonzales v. Carhart* and *Gonzales v. Planned Parenthood*, the partial-birth abortion decisions from the

Eighth and Ninth Circuits. This chapter reviews the two cases and discusses the arguments put forth by the parties. It also provides background information on the PBABA.

Chapter 7 - The term "partial-birth abortion" refers generally to an abortion procedure where the fetus is removed intact from a woman's body. The procedure is described by the medical community as "intact dilation and evacuation" or "dilation and extraction" ("D & X") depending on the presentation of the fetus. Intact dilation and evacuation involves a vertex or "head first" presentation, the induced dilation of the cervix, the collapsing of the skull, and the extraction of the entire fetus through the cervix. D & X involves a breech or "feet first" presentation, the induced dilation of the cervix, the removal of the fetal body through the cervix, the collapsing of the skull, and the extraction of the fetus through the cervix.

Since 1995, at least thirty-one states have enacted laws banning partial-birth abortions. Although many of these laws have not taken effect because of temporary or permanent injunctions, they remain contentious to both pro-life advocates and those who support a woman's right to choose. This chapter discusses the U.S. Supreme Court's decision in *Stenberg v. Carhart*, a case involving the constitutionality of Nebraska's partial-birth abortion ban statute. In *Stenberg*, the Court invalidated the Nebraska statute because it lacked an exception for the performance of the partial-birth abortion procedure when necessary to protect the health of the mother, and because it imposed an undue burden on a woman's ability to have an abortion.

This chapter also reviews various legislative attempts to restrict partial-birth abortions during the 106th, 107th, and 108th Congresses. S. 3, the Partial-Birth Abortion Ban Act of 2003, was signed by the President on November 4, 2003. On April 18, 2007, the Court upheld the act, finding that, as a facial matter, it is not unconstitutionally vague and does not impose an undue burden on a woman's right to terminate her pregnancy. In reaching its conclusion in *Gonzales v. Carhart*, the Court distinguished the federal statute from the Nebraska law at issue in *Stenberg*.

Chapter 8 - State laws that require parental involvement in a pregnant minor's abortion decision have gained greater visibility in light of recent attempts by Congress to criminalize the interstate transport of a minor to obtain an abortion. At least forty-three states have enacted statutes that require a minor to seek either parental notification or parental consent before obtaining an abortion. This chapter discusses the validity of state parental involvement laws in the context of *Planned Parenthood of Southeastern Pennsylvania v. Casey*, *Ayotte v. Planned Parenthood of Northern New England*, and other U.S. Supreme Court cases that address a minor's right to choose whether to terminate her pregnancy. The report reviews the various state parental involvement law provisions, such as judicial bypass procedures and exceptions for medical emergencies. The report also highlights recent federal parental involvement legislation and provides a survey of current state parental involvement laws.

In: Abortion: Legislative and Legal Issues   ISBN: 978-1-60741-522-0
Editor: Kevin G. Nolan   © 2010 Nova Science Publishers, Inc.

Chapter 1

ABORTION LAW DEVELOPMENT: A BRIEF OVERVIEW[*]

Jon O. Shimabukuro

SUMMARY

In *Roe v. Wade*, 410 U.S. 113 (1973), the U.S. Supreme Court determined that the Constitution protects a woman's decision whether or not to terminate her pregnancy. In a companion case, *Doe v. Bolton*, 410 U.S. 179 (1973), the Court held further that a state may not unduly burden a woman's fundamental right to abortion by prohibiting or substantially limiting access to the means of effectuating her decision. Rather than settle the issue, the Court's decisions kindled heated debate and precipitated a variety of governmental actions at the national, state and local levels designed either to nullify the rulings or hinder their effectuation. These governmental regulations have, in turn, spawned further litigation in which resulting judicial refinements in the law have been no more successful in dampening the controversy.

The law with respect to abortion in mid-19th century America followed the common law of England in all but a few states. By the time of the Civil War, a number of states had begun to revise their statutes in order to prohibit abortion

---

[*] This is an edited, reformatted and augmented version of a CRS Report for Congress publication, Report 95-724, dated January 15, 2009.

at all stages of gestation, with various exceptions for therapeutic abortions. The year 1967 marked the first victory of an abortion reform movement with the passage of liberalizing legislation in Colorado. The legislation was based on the Model Penal Code. Between 1967 and 1973, approximately one-third of the states had adopted, either in whole or in part, the Model Penal Code's provisions allowing abortion in instances other than where only the mother's life was in danger. Between 1968 and 1972, abortion statutes of many states were challenged on the grounds of vagueness, violation of the fundamental right of privacy, and denial of equal protection. In 1973, the Court ruled in *Roe* and *Doe* that Texas and Georgia statutes regulating abortion interfered to an unconstitutional extent with a woman's right to decide whether to terminate her pregnancy. The decisions rested upon the conclusion that the Fourteenth Amendment right of personal privacy encompassed a woman's decision whether to carry a pregnancy to term.

The Supreme Court's decisions in *Roe* and *Doe* did not address a number of important abortionrelated issues which have been raised subsequently by state actions seeking to restrict the scope of the Court's rulings. These include the issues of informed consent, spousal consent, parental consent, and reporting requirements. In addition, *Roe* and *Doe* never resolved the question of what, if any, type of abortion procedures may be required or prohibited by statute. In 1989, the Court indicated in *Webster v. Reproductive Health Services*, 492 U.S. 490, that, while it was not overruling *Roe* and *Doe*, it was willing to apply a less stringent standard of review to state restrictions respecting a woman's right to an abortion. Then, in 1992, in *Planned Parenthood of Southeastern Pennsylvania v. Casey*, 505 U.S. 833 (1992), the Court rejected specifically *Roe*'s strict scrutiny standard and adopted the undue burden analysis. In 2000, in *Stenberg v. Carhart*, 530 U.S. 914 (2000), the Court determined that a Nebraska statute prohibiting the performance of "partial-birth" abortions was unconstitutional. In 2007, however, the Court upheld the federal Partial-Birth Abortion Ban Act of 2003 in *Gonzales v. Carhart*, 550 U.S. 124 (2007). In upholding the federal act, the Court distinguished between the federal measure and the Nebraska statute.

INTRODUCTION

In *Roe v. Wade*, the U.S. Supreme Court determined that the Constitution protects a woman's decision whether or not to terminate her pregnancy.[1] In a companion case, *Doe v. Bolton*, the Court held further that a state may not unduly burden a woman's fundamental right to abortion by prohibiting or substantially limiting access to the means of effectuating her decision.[2] Rather than settle the issue, the Court's decisions kindled heated debate and precipitated a variety of governmental actions at the national, state and local levels designed either to nullify the rulings or hinder their effectuation. These governmental regulations have, in turn, spawned further litigation in which resulting judicial refinements in the law have been no more successful in dampening the controversy.

This chapter offers an overview of the development of abortion law from 1973 to the present. Beginning with a brief discussion of the historical background, the report analyzes the leading Supreme Court decisions over the past 34 years, emphasizing particularly the landmark decisions in *Roe* and *Doe*, the Court's shift in direction in *Webster v. Reproductive Health Services* and *Planned Parenthood of Southeastern Pennsylvania v. Casey*, and the Court's most recent decision on abortion, *Carhart v. Gonzales*.[3] The Court's decisions on the constitutionality of restricting public funding for abortion are also discussed.

I. DEVELOPMENT AND STATUS OF THE LAW PRIOR TO 1973

The law with respect to abortion in mid-19th century America followed existing common law of England in all but a few states.[4] Thus, no indictment would occur for aborting a fetus of a consenting female prior to "quickening." But, by the time of the Civil War, an influential antiabortion movement began to affect legislation by inducing states to add to or revise their statutes in order to prohibit abortion at all stages of gestation. By 1910, every state had anti-abortion laws, except Kentucky whose courts judicially declared abortions to be illegal. In 1967, forty-nine states and the District of Columbia classified the crime of abortion as a felony. The concept of "quickening" was no longer used to determine criminal liability but was retained in some states to set punishment. Nontherapeutic abortions were essentially unlawful. The states varied in their exceptions for therapeutic abortions. Forty-two states permitted abortions only if necessary to save the life of the mother. Other states allowed abortion to save a woman from "serious permanent bodily injury" or her "life and health." Three states allowed abortions that were not "unlawfully performed" or that were not "without lawful justification", leaving interpretation of those standards to the courts.

This, however, represented the high water mark in restrictive abortion laws in the United States, for 1967 saw the first victory of an abortion reform movement with the passage of liberalizing legislation in Colorado. The movement had started in the early 1950s and centered its efforts on a proposed criminal abortion statute developed by the American Law Institute as part of its Model Penal Code that would allow abortions when childbirth posed grave danger to the physical or mental health of a woman, when there was high likelihood of fetal abnormality, or when pregnancy resulted from rape or incest.

Between 1967 and the Supreme Court's 1973 decisions in *Roe* and *Doe*, approximately one-third of the states had adopted, either in whole or in part, the Model Penal Code's provisions allowing abortions in instances other than where only the mother's life was in danger. Also, by the end of 1970, four states (Alaska, Hawaii, New York, and Washington) had repealed criminal penalties for abortions performed in early pregnancy by a licensed physician, subject to stated procedural and health requirements.

The first U.S. Supreme Court decision dealing with abortion was rendered in 1971. In *United States v. Vuitch*, the Court denied a vagueness challenge to the District of Columbia abortion statute.[5] The net effect of the *Vuitch* decision was to expand the availability of abortions under the D.C. law's provision allowing abortions where "necessary for the preservation of the mother's ... health."

II. THE SUPREME COURT'S 1973 ABORTION RULINGS

Between 1968 and 1972, the constitutionality of restrictive abortion statutes of many states was challenged on the grounds of vagueness, violation of the fundamental right of privacy, and denial of equal protection. These challenges met with mixed success in the lower courts. However, in 1973, the Supreme Court issued its rulings in *Roe v. Wade* and *Doe v. Bolton*. In those cases the Court found that Texas and Georgia statutes regulating abortion interfered to an unconstitutional extent with a woman's right to decide whether to terminate her pregnancy. The Texas statute forbade all abortions not necessary "for the purpose of saving the life of the mother." The Georgia enactment permitted abortions when continued pregnancy seriously threatened the woman's life or health, when the fetus was very likely to have severe birth defects, or when the pregnancy resulted from rape. The Georgia statute required, however, that abortions be performed only at accredited hospitals and only after approval by a hospital committee and two consulting physicians.

The Court's decisions were delivered by Justice Blackmun for himself and six other Justices. Justices White and Rehnquist dissented. The Court ruled that states may not categorically proscribe abortions by making their performance a crime, and that states may not make abortions unnecessarily difficult to obtain by prescribing elaborate procedural guidelines. The constitutional basis for the decisions rested upon the conclusion that the Fourteenth Amendment right of personal privacy embraced a woman's decision whether to carry a pregnancy to term. The Court noted that its prior decisions had "found at least the roots of ... [a] guarantee of personal privacy" in various amendments to the Constitution or their penumbras (i.e., protected offshoots) and characterized the right to privacy as grounded in "the Fourteenth Amendment's concept of personal liberty and restrictions upon State action."[6] Regarding the scope of that right, the Court stated that it included "only personal rights that can be deemed 'fundamental' or 'implicit in the concept of ordered liberty'" and "bears some extension to activities related to marriage, procreation, contraception, family relationship, and child rearing and education."[7] Such a right, the Court concluded, "is broad enough to encompass a woman's decision whether or not to terminate her pregnancy."[8]

With respect to protection of the right against state interference, the Court held that since the right of personal privacy is a fundamental right, only a "compelling state interest" could justify its limitation by a state. Thus while it recognized the legitimacy of the state interest in protecting maternal health and the preservation of the fetus' potential life, and the existence of a rational connection between these two interests and the state's anti-abortion law, the Court held these interests insufficient to justify an absolute ban on abortions.[9] Instead, the Court emphasized the durational nature of pregnancy and held the state's interests to be sufficiently compelling to permit curtailment or prohibition of abortion only during specified stages of pregnancy. The High Court concluded that until the end of the first trimester, an abortion is no more dangerous to maternal health than childbirth itself, and found that "[W]ith respect to the State's important and legitimate interest in the health of the mother, the 'compelling' point, in light of present medical knowledge, is at approximately the end of the first trimester."[10] Only after the first trimester does the state's interest in protecting maternal health provide a sufficient basis to justify state regulation of abortion, and then only to protect this interest.[11]

The "compelling" point with respect to the state's interest in the potential life of the fetus "is at viability." Following viability, the state's interest permits it to regulate and even proscribe an abortion except when necessary, in appropriate medical judgment, for the preservation of the life or health of the mother.[12] The Court defined viability as the point at which the fetus is "potentially able to live outside the mother's womb, albeit with artificial aid."[13] It summarized its holding as follows:

(a) For the stage prior to approximately the end of the first trimester [of pregnancy], the abortion decision and its effectuation must be left to the medical judgment of the pregnant woman's attending physician.

(b) For the stage subsequent to approximately the end of the first trimester, the State, in promoting its interest in the health of the mother, may, if it chooses, regulate the abortion procedure in ways that are reasonably related to maternal health.

(c) For the stage subsequent to viability, the State, in promoting its interest in the potentiality of human life may, if it chooses, regulate, and even proscribe, abortion except where it is necessary, in appropriate medical judgment, for the preservation of the life or health of the mother.[14]

In *Doe*, the Court reiterated its holding in *Roe* that the basic decision of when an abortion is proper rests with the pregnant mother and her physician, but extended *Roe* by warning that just as states may not prevent abortion by making their performance a crime, states may not make abortions unreasonably difficult to obtain by prescribing elaborate procedural barriers. In *Doe*, the Court struck down state requirements that abortions be performed in licensed hospitals; that abortions be approved beforehand by a hospital committee; and that two physicians concur in the abortion decision.[15] The Court appeared to note, however, that this would not apply to a statute that protected the religious or moral beliefs of denominational hospitals and their employees.[16]

The Court in *Roe* also dealt with the question whether a fetus is a person and thereby protected under the Fourteenth Amendment and other provisions of the Constitution. The Court indicated that the Constitution never specifically defines, "person," but added that in nearly all the sections where the word person appears, "the use of the word is such that it has application only postnatally. None indicates with any assurance, that it has any possible pre-natal application."[17] The Court emphasized that, given the fact that in the major part of the 19th century prevailing legal abortion practices were far freer than today, the Court was persuaded "that the word 'person,' as used in the Fourteenth Amendment, does not include the unborn."[18]

The Court did not, however, resolve the question of when life actually begins. While noting the divergence of thinking on this issue, it instead articulated the legal concept of "viability," defined as the point at which the fetus is potentially able to live outside the womb, although the fetus may require artificial aid.[19] Many other questions were also not addressed in *Roe* and *Doe*, but instead formed the grist for a burgeoning book of post-*Roe* litigation.

III. PUBLIC FUNDING OF ABORTIONS

Two categories of public funding cases have been heard and decided by the Supreme Court: those involving (1) funding restrictions for nontherapeutic (elective) abortions; and (2) funding limitations for therapeutic (medically necessary) abortions.

1. The 1977 Trilogy—Restrictions on Public Funding of Nontherapeutic or Elective Abortions

The Supreme Court, in three related decisions, ruled on the question whether the Medicaid statute or the Constitution requires public funding of nontherapeutic (elective) abortions for indigent women or access to public facilities for the performance of such abortions.[20] The Court held that the states have neither a statutory nor a constitutional obligation in this regard.

In *Beal v. Doe*, the Court held that nothing in the language or legislative history of Title XIX of the Social Security Act (Medicaid) requires a participating state to fund every medical procedure falling within the delineated categories of medical care. The Court ruled that it was not inconsistent with the act's goals to refuse to fund unnecessary medical services. However, the Court did indicate that Title XIX left a state free to include coverage for nontherapeutic abortions should it choose to do so. Similarly, in *Maher v. Roe*, the Court held that the Equal Protection Clause of the U.S. Constitution does not require a state participating in the Medicaid program to pay expenses incident to nontherapeutic abortions simply because the state has made a policy choice to pay expenses incident to childbirth. More particularly, Connecticut's policy of favoring childbirth over abortion was held not to impinge upon the fundamental right of privacy recognized in *Roe*, which protects a woman from undue interference in her decision to terminate a pregnancy. Finally, in *Poelker v. Doe*, the Court upheld a municipal regulation that denied indigent pregnant women nontherapeutic abortions at public hospitals. It also held that staffing those hospitals with personnel opposed to the performance of abortions did not violate the Equal Protection Clause of the Constitution. *Poelker*, however, did not deal with the question of private hospitals and their authority to prohibit abortion services.

2. Public Funding of Therapeutic or Medically Necessary Abortions

The 1977 Supreme Court decisions left open the question whether Federal law, such as the Hyde Amendment, or similar state laws, could validly prohibit governmental funding of therapeutic abortions.

The Court ruled 5-4 that the Hyde Amendment's abortion funding restrictions were constitutional. The majority found that the Hyde Amendment neither violated the Due Process or Equal Protection guarantees of the Fifth Amendment nor the Establishment [of religion] Clause of the First Amendment. The Court also upheld the right of a state participating in the Medicaid program to fund only those medically necessary abortions for which it received Federal reimbursement.[21] In companion cases raising similar issues, the Court held that a State of Illinois statutory funding restriction comparable to the Federal Hyde Amendment also did not contravene the constitutional restrictions of the Equal Protection Clause of the Fourteenth Amendment.[22] The Court's rulings mean there is no statutory or constitutional obligation of the states or the Federal Government to fund all medically necessary abortions.

IV. SUPREME COURT DECISIONS SUBSEQUENT TO *ROE* AND *DOE* INVOLVING THE SUBSTANTIVE RIGHT TO ABORTION

Informed Consent/Waiting Periods

In *Planned Parenthood v. Danforth*, the Court held that informed consent statutes, which require a doctor to obtain the written consent of a woman after informing her of the dangers of abortion and possible alternatives, are constitutional if the requirements are related to maternal health and are not overbearing.[23] The fact that the informed consent laws must define their requirements very narrowly in order to be constitutional was later confirmed the Supreme Court in 1979.[24] The requirements of an informed consent statute must also be narrowly drawn so as not to unduly interfere with the physician-patient relationship, although the type of information required to be given to a woman of necessity may vary according to the trimester of her pregnancy.

In *City of Akron v. Akron Center for Reproductive Health, Inc.*, along with various other provisions, the Court struck down the informed written consent section of the ordinance.[25] This provision required that the attending doctor inform the woman "of the status of her pregnancy, the development of her fetus, the date of possible viability, the physical and emotional complications that may result from an abortion, and the availability of agencies to provide her with assistance and information with respect to birth control, adoption, and childbirth."[26] The attending physician was also required to tell the patient of the risks involved and any other information which in the physician's medical judgment would be critical to her decision of whether to terminate the pregnancy. The Court found this informed consent requirement to be constitutionally unacceptable because it essentially gave the government unreviewable authority over what information was to be given a woman before she decided whether to have an abortion. It was also objectionable because it intruded upon the discretion of the pregnant woman's doctor.[27]

The Supreme Court also invalidated the 24-hour waiting period, holding that the City of Akron had not shown that any legitimate state interest was being served "by an arbitrary and inflexible waiting period."

Spousal/Parental Consent

In addition to informed consent, the Court in *Danforth*, found that spousal consent statutes, which require a written statement by the father of the fetus affirming his consent to the abortion, are unconstitutional if the statutes allow the husband to unilaterally prohibit the abortion in the first trimester. It should be noted that on the same day that the Supreme Court decided *Danforth*, it also summarily affirmed the lower court decision in *Coe v. Gerstein*, which held unconstitutional a spousal consent law regardless of the stage of the woman's pregnancy.[28]

With respect to parental consent statutes, the Supreme Court held in *Danforth* that statutes which allow a parent or guardian to absolutely prohibit an abortion to be performed on a minor child were unconstitutional. Subsequently, in *Bellotti v. Baird*, the Court ruled that while a state may require a minor to obtain parental consent, it must also provide an alternative procedure to procure authorization if parental consent is denied or the minor does not want to seek it.[29] *Bellotti* thus entitles a minor to some proceeding which allows her to prove her ability to make an informed decision independent of her parents or, even if she is incapable of making the decision, at least showing that the abortion would be in her best interests.

In *City of Akron*, the Court invalidated the provision in the Akron ordinance which prohibited a doctor from performing an abortion on an unemancipated minor unless the doctor obtained "the informed written consent of one of her parents or her legal guardian" or unless the minor herself obtained "an order from a court having jurisdiction over her that her abortion be performed or induced."[30] The Court relied on its earlier rulings in *Danforth* and *Bellotti* to conclude that the City of Akron could "not make a blanket determination that all minors under the age of 15 are too immature to make this decision or that an abortion never may be in the minor's best interests without parental approval."[31] Moreover, the Akron ordinance's provision concerning parental approval did not create expressly the alternative judicial procedure required by *Bellotti*. Thus, the ordinance's consent provision had to fall because it foreclosed any possibility for "case-by-case evaluations of the maturity of pregnant minors."[32]

In *Planned Parenthood Association of Kansas City, Missouri Inc. v. Ashcroft*, the Supreme Court upheld Missouri's parental consent requirement.[33] It distinguished the provision involved here from that challenged in *City of Akron*. The Missouri requirement, unlike the Akron one, did provide an alternative procedure by which a pregnant immature minor could show in court that she was sufficiently mature to make the abortion decision herself or that, despite her immaturity, an abortion would in her best interests.

Parental Notification

In 1981, the Court upheld a Utah state law making it a crime for doctors to perform an abortion on an unemancipated, dependent minor without notifying her parents. In *H. L. v. Matheson*, a 6-3 decision, the Court examined the narrow question of the facial constitutionality of a statute requiring a physician to give notice to parents, "if possible," prior to performing an abortion on their minor daughter: (a) when the girl is living with and dependent upon her parents; (b) when she is not emancipated by marriage or otherwise; and (c) when she has made no claim or showing as to her maturity or as to her relationship with her parents.[34] The Supreme Court cited the interest in preserving family integrity and protecting adolescents in allowing states to require that parents be informed that their daughter is seeking an abortion, and emphasized that the statute in question did not give a veto power over the minor's abortion decision. The Court rejected the minor woman's contention that abortion was being singled out for special treatment in contrast to other surgical procedures, like childbirth, which do not require parental notice.

In 1987, an equally divided Supreme Court, without opinion, let stand a 7th Circuit Court of Appeals decision invalidating an Illinois law that required teenagers to notify their parents prior to obtaining an abortion.[35] The tie vote meant that the ruling set no nationwide precedent. There are other states with parental notification laws similar to the one in Illinois.

During its October 1989 Term, the Court decided two cases involving challenges to the constitutionality of state parental notification laws. In *Hodgson v. Minnesota*, the Court held 5 to 4 that a Minnesota requirement for notice to be given to *both* parents prior to a minor's having an abortion was unconstitutional unless the state legislature provided for an alternative hearing in court, i.e., a judicial bypass procedure.[36]

In *Ohio v. Akron Center for Reproductive Health*, a 6-3 decision, the Court upheld an Ohio statute requiring notice to one parent.[37] The Court concluded that the statute, which included a judicial bypass procedure, was consistent with the statutes upheld in *Danforth*, *Bellotti*, *Ashcroft*, and *Akron*: "it is a corollary to the greater intrusiveness of consent statutes that a bypass procedure that will suffice for a consent statute will suffice also for a notice statute."[38] Although the Court upheld the Ohio statute, it made clear that it was not deciding whether a parental notification statute must always include a judicial bypass procedure to be constitutional.[39]

In *Lambert v. Wicklund*, a 1997 case involving a Montana parental notification statute, the Court again declined to consider whether a parental notification requirement must include a judicial bypass procedure.[40] The Court's unwillingness to consider the matter has led to disagreement among some of the U.S. Courts of Appeals.[41]

Miscellaneous

1. Reporting requirements

The Court in *Danforth* ruled that statutes requiring doctors and health facilities to provide information to states regarding each abortion performed are constitutional. The Court specified, however, that these reporting requirements must relate to maternal health, remain confidential, and may not be overbearing.[42]

In *Ashcroft*, the Court upheld the pathology report requirement. This provision was "related to generally accepted medical standards" and "further[s] important health-related State concerns."[43] The Court further found that the cost of the tissue examination "does not significantly burden a pregnant woman's abortion decision."[44]

2. Advertisement of Abortion Services

The Supreme Court held in *Bigelow v. Virginia*, that a state may not proscribe advertising regarding the availability of an abortion or abortion-related services in another state.[45] The Court found that the statute in question was unconstitutional because the State of Virginia, where the advertisement appeared, had only a minimal interest in the health and medical practices of New York, the state in which the legal abortion services were located.

3. Abortions by Nonphysicians

In *Connecticut v. Menillo*, the Supreme Court ruled that state statutes similar to the Texas law challenged in *Roe* were constitutional to the extent that the statutes forbid nonphysicians from performing abortions.[46] The *Roe* decision made it clear that a state could not interfere with a woman's decision, made in consultation with and upon the advice of her doctor, to have an abortion in the first trimester of her pregnancy. The *Menillo* Court found that pre-*Roe* restrictive abortion laws were still enforceable against nonphysicians.[47]

4. Locus of Abortions

In *City of Akron*, the Court invalidated the challenged Akron ordinance provision relating to where abortions can be performed. The requirement stated that any second trimester abortion had to be performed in a full-service hospital. The accreditation of these facilities required compliance with comprehensive standards governing an extensive variety of health and surgical services. The result was that abortions under this section of the Akron ordinance could not be performed in outpatient facilities that were not part of an acute-care, full-service hospital. The Court found this restriction unconstitutional, noting that the possibility of having to travel to find facilities could result in both financial expense and added risk to a woman's health.[48] The Court also cited changed medical circumstances, and the availability of safer procedures for performing second trimester abortions since *Roe*, for its conclusion that the Akron hospitalization requirement imposed an unreasonable burden on a woman's right to an abortion.

In *Ashcroft*, the Court invalidated Missouri's second trimester hospitalization requirement by the same 6-3 vote as in *City of Akron*. It said its decision and rationale in *City of Akron* were controlling.

In *Simopoulos v. Virginia*, the Supreme Court ruled that Virginia's mandatory hospitalization requirement for second trimester abortions was constitutional.[49] The Court distinguished the requirement in question from those it invalidated in *City of Akron* and *Ashcroft* which mandated that all second trimester abortions be performed in acute-care facilities. In *Simopoulos,* the Court said that, in contrast, the Virginia law did not require that second trimester abortions be performed exclusively in full-service hospitals. The determination upholding the Virginia provision actually turned on the definition of "hospital." The Court wrote: "Under Virginia's hospitalization requirement, outpatient surgical hospitals may qualify for licensing as 'hospitals' in which second-trimester abortions lawfully may be performed."[50]

5. Viability, Fetal Testing, and Disposal of Fetal Remains

The Supreme Court's articulation of the concept of viability has required further elaboration, particularly with regard to the critical question of who defines at what point a fetus has reached viability. In *Roe*, the Court defined viability as the point at which the fetus is "potentially able to live outside the mother's womb, albeit with artificial aid."[51] Such potentiality, however, must be for "meaningful life" and this cannot encompass simply momentary survival.[52] The Court also noted that while viability is usually placed at about 28 weeks, it can occur earlier and essentially left the point flexible for anticipated advances in medical skill. Finally, *Roe* stressed the central role of the pregnant woman's doctor, emphasizing that "the abortion decision in all its aspects is inherently, and primarily, a medical decision."[53]

Similar themes were stressed in *Danforth*, in which a Missouri law, which defined viability as "that stage of fetal development when the life of the unborn child may be continued indefinitely outside the womb by natural or artificial life support systems", was attacked as an attempt to advance the point of viability to an earlier stage of gestation. The Court disagreed, finding the statutory definition consistent with *Roe*. It reemphasized that viability is "a matter of medical judgment, skill, and technical ability" and that *Roe* meant to preserve the flexibility of the term.[54] Moreover, the *Danforth* Court held that "it is not the proper function of the legislature or the courts to place viability, which is essentially a medical concept, at a specific point in the gestation period. The time when viability is achieved may vary with each pregnancy, and the determination of whether a particular fetus is viable is, and must be, a matter for the judgment of the attending physician."[55] The physician's central role in determining viability, and the lack of such definitional authority in the legislatures and courts, was reaffirmed by the Court in *Colautti v. Franklin*.[56]

In *Danforth*, the Court ruled that fetal protection statutes were generally overbroad and unconstitutional if they pertained to pre-viable fetuses. Such statutes require a doctor performing an abortion to use available means and medical skills to save the life of the fetus. In *Colautti*, the Supreme Court held subsequently that such fetal protection statutes could only apply to viable fetuses and that the statute must be precise in setting forth the standard for determining viability. In addition, the Court in *Colautti* stressed that in order to meet the constitutional test of sufficient certainty, fetal protection laws had to define whether a doctor's paramount duty was to the patient or whether the physician had to balance the possible danger to the patient against the increased odds of fetal survival.[57]

In *Ashcroft*, the Court found that the second-physician requirement during the third trimester was permissible under the Constitution because it "reasonably furthers the State's compelling interest in protecting the lives of viable fetuses ... ".[58]

In *City of Akron*, the Court ruled that the portion of the Akron ordinance requiring that physicians performing abortions see to it that the remains of the unborn child be disposed of "in a humane and sanitary" way was void for vagueness. The level of uncertainty present was unacceptable in a situation such as this where there was the prospect of criminal liability being imposed.[59]

V. SETTING THE STAGE FOR CASEY: WEBSTER V. REPRODUCTIVE HEALTH SERVICES

The 1983 Supreme Court decisions in *City of Akron*, *Ashcroft*, and *Simopoulos* settled questions relating to hospital requirements for second trimester abortions, informed consent requirements, waiting periods, parental notification and consent, and disposal of fetal remains. The Supreme Court reaffirmed its decision in *Roe* and its intention to continue to follow the trimester framework balancing a woman's constitutional right to decide whether to terminate a pregnancy with the State's interest in protecting potential life. The State's interest in protecting potential life becomes "compelling" at the point of viability, i.e., when the fetus can exist outside of a woman's womb either on its own or through artificial means. The definition of viability is the one used by the Court in its *Roe* decision in 1973. Again, in 1986, the Court reaffirmed *Roe* in *Thornburgh v. American College of Obstetricians and Gynecologists*.[60]

In 1989, the Supreme Court upheld the constitutionality of the State of Missouri's abortion statute in *Webster* v. *Reproductive Health Services*.[61] In this 5-4 decision, while the majority did not overrule *Roe*, it indicated that it was willing to apply a less stringent standard of review to state restrictions on abortion. *Webster* made it clear that state legislatures have considerable discretion to pass restrictive legislation in the future, with the likelihood that such laws would probably pass constitutional muster.

The main provisions in the 1986 Missouri law upheld by the Court included (1) barring public employees from performing or assisting in abortions not necessary to save the life of the mother; (2) barring the use of public buildings for performing abortions, despite the fact that there were no public monies involved (e.g., a building situated on public land); and (3) requiring physicians believing a woman desiring an abortion to be at least 20 weeks pregnant to perform tests to determine whether the fetus is viable. The Court's majority chose not to rule on the Missouri law's Preamble language which described life as beginning at conception with constitutional protections attaching at that point. Chief Justice Rehnquist, writing for the

Court, said that the Preamble by its terms did not regulate abortion, and that it was an expression of a value judgment favoring childbirth over abortion. He noted that the Court in past cases has emphasized that *Roe* implies no limitation on a State's authority to make such a value judgment. The *Webster* ruling was narrow in that it did not affect private doctors' offices or clinics, where most abortions are performed. Its significance derives more from the rationales articulated by the five justices regarding how abortion restrictions would be reviewed in the future. *Webster* set the stage for the Court's 1992 decision in *Casey*.

The majority opinion in *Webster* became splintered when the justices reviewed the Missouri provision respecting a doctor's testing for viability at 20 weeks of pregnancy. While the five justices (Rehnquist, White, Kennedy, Scalia, and O'Connor) agreed that the provision was constitutional, they had different reasons for so holding. Chief Justice Rehnquist, joined by Justices White and Kennedy, agreed with the district court and court of appeals that the required tests added increased costs to obtaining a second trimester abortion. In *Roe*, the Court had held that in the second trimester of pregnancy, the state could regulate abortion only in the interests of the health of the mother; and that it is only after viability (when the fetus can exist outside the womb on its own or through artificial means) that states are allowed to actually restrict abortions in the interests of protecting the fetus, i.e., potential life. A plurality disagreed with the *Roe* reasoning in this context and with the trimester framework upon which it is predicated. Chief Justice Rehnquist and Justices White and Kennedy instead proposed to apply a new standard of review for state abortion restrictions: whether the state regulation "permissibly furthers the State's interest in protecting potential human life". They concluded that the Missouri law's viability testing requirements did and therefore found that provision to be constitutional. The plurality put in doubt the whole concept of "viability" as the basis of determining when the state's interest in regulating abortion pertains: "we do not see why the State's interest in protecting potential human life should come into existence only at the point of viability, and there should therefore be a rigid line allowing state regulation after viability but prohibiting it before viability."

However, because the Missouri law did not limit abortions prior to viability, the plurality did not believe it was necessary to consider overruling *Roe*. Also, Chief Justice Rehnquist stated that the Missouri statute was different from the Texas statute challenged in *Roe*—the latter being a criminal abortion law. The plurality stated that it was instead modifying and narrowing

Roe for application in future cases involving challenges to the constitutionality of state abortion restrictions.

Justice Scalia wrote a separate concurrence because he believed that the Court did not go far enough. He would have overruled *Roe* explicitly. Justice O'Connor, also a part of the majority, wrote a separate concurrence as well but for different reasons. She was not ready to go as far as Justice Scalia and overrule *Roe*; nor was she prepared to join the plurality and dispense with the trimester framework of *Roe* at this time. She stated in concurrence that the trimester system was problematic, but that there was no need to modify it in *Webster* because the validity of the Missouri law's viability provision could be decided under existing precedent, i.e., *Roe* and succeeding decisions. She applied a standard of "undue burden" and found the restriction to be constitutional: "requiring the performance of examinations and tests useful to determining whether a fetus is viable, when viability is possible, and when it would not be medically imprudent to do so, does not impose an undue burden on a woman's abortion decision."

VI. A SHIFT IN DIRECTION: PLANNED PARENTHOOD OF SOUTHEASTERN PENNSYLVANIA V. CASEY

In 1991, the Court in *Rust* v. *Sullivan* upheld on both statutory and constitutional grounds HHS' Title X regulations restricting recipients of Federal family planning funding from counseling women about the option of abortion.[62] This case can better be described as one involving a challenge to First Amendment free speech rights than to the constitutionally guaranteed substantive right to an abortion; however, following its earlier public funding cases (*Maher* v. *Roe* and *Harris* v. *McRae*) as precedent, the Court did conclude that a woman's right to an abortion was not burdened by these regulations. The Court reasoned that there was no such violation because the Government has no duty to subsidize an activity simply because it is constitutionally protected and because a woman is "in no worse position than if Congress had never enacted Title X."

Both *Webster* and *Rust* energized legislative activity, the former at both the Federal and state levels, and the latter only at the Federal level. Some of the state legislative proposals that have become law have been challenged in the courts, e.g., Pennsylvania, Guam, Louisiana, and Utah. The Pennsylvania case, *Planned Parenthood of Southeastern Pennsylvania v. Casey*, was decided by the U.S. Supreme Court on June 29, 1992.[63] In a highly fractionated 5-4 decision, the Court reaffirmed the basic constitutional right to an abortion while simultaneously allowing some new restrictions. Justices O'Connor, Kennedy and Souter wrote the plurality opinion, and they were joined in part by Justices Stevens and Blackmun. Chief Justice Rehnquist and Justices White, Scalia and Thomas dissented. The Court refused to overrule *Roe*, and the plurality explained at length why it was important to follow precedent. "The Constitution serves human values, and while the effect of reliance on *Roe* cannot be exactly measured, neither can the certain cost of overruling *Roe* for people who have ordered their thinking and living around that case be dismissed."[64] At the same time, the plurality indicated that state laws which contained an outright ban on abortion would be unconstitutional. Nevertheless, the Court abandoned the trimester framework articulated in *Roe* and the strict scrutiny standard of judicial review of abortion restrictions. Instead, it adopted a new analysis, "undue burden." Courts will now need to ask the question whether a state abortion restriction has the effect of imposing an "undue burden" on a woman's right to obtain an abortion. "Undue burden" was defined as a "substantial obstacle in the path of a woman seeking an abortion of a nonviable fetus."[65]

The Court applied this new analysis to the Pennsylvania statute and concluded that four of the provisions did not impose an undue burden on the right to abortion and were constitutional. Those provisions upheld were the 24-hour waiting period; informed consent; parental consent by minors with a judicial bypass; and reporting requirements. The Court also upheld the "medical emergency" definition under which other requirements can be waived. The spousal notification provision, requiring a married woman to tell her husband she intends to have an abortion, did not survive the "undue burden" test, and it was struck down as being unconstitutional. The dissenters would have upheld all of the provisions in the Pennsylvania law as well as overturn *Roe* itself. Justices Stevens and Blackmun wrote separate opinions. They joined the plurality in holding the spousal notification provision unconstitutional. Justice Stevens was vague concerning whether he was accepting the new "undue burden" analysis, but he did indicate that his application of it might be more stringent than the plurality's. On the other hand, Justice Blackmun stated that he would retain the analysis used in *Roe*, i.e., strict scrutiny.

The Court's decision in *Casey* was significant because it appeared that the new standard of review would allow more state restrictions to pass constitutional muster. The decision was also noteworthy because the Court found that the state's interest in protecting the potentiality of human life extended throughout the course of the pregnancy, and thus the state could regulate, even to the point of favoring childbirth over abortion, from the outset. Under *Roe*, which utilized the trimester framework, during the first trimester of pregnancy, the woman's decision to terminate her pregnancy was reached in consultation between her and her doctor with virtually no state involvement. Also, under *Roe*, abortion was a "fundamental right" that could not be restricted by the state except to serve a "compelling" state interest. *Roe's* strict scrutiny form of review resulted in most state regulations being invalidated during the first two trimesters of pregnancy. The "undue burden" standard seems to allow more regulation during that period. This is evident from the Court's overruling, in part, two of its earlier decisions which had followed *Roe*: *City of Akron* and *Thornburgh v. American College of Obstetricians and Gynecologists*.[66] In those cases, the Court, applying strict scrutiny, struck down 24-hour waiting periods and informed consent provisions. In contrast, the Court in *Casey* upheld similar provisions after applying the undue burden standard.

VII. APPLYING CASEY: STENBERG V. CARHART AND GONZALES V. CARHART

Following *Casey*, the Court appeared reluctant to review another abortion case. Between 1992 and 1993, the Court declined to hear appeals in three abortion cases.[67] Contrary decisions by the U.S. Courts of Appeals regarding the validity of state statutes prohibiting "partial-birth" abortions, as well as congressional interest in enacting federal partial-birth legislation may have prompted the Court to decide *Stenberg v. Carhart*.[68]

The term "partial-birth abortion" refers generally to a method of abortion that involves the removal of the fetal body, with the exception of the skull, intact.[69] "Dilation and evacuation" or "D & E" is the most common abortion procedure.[70] D & E involves the dilation of the cervix and the dismemberment of the fetus inside the uterus. Fetal parts are later removed from the uterus either with forceps or by suction.

The partial-birth abortion procedure is a variation on the D & E procedure. The procedure begins with the induced dilation of the cervix. If the fetus presents head first, the doctor will collapse the skull and remove the entire fetus through the cervix. This procedure is called "intact D & E" by the medical community.[71] If the fetus presents feet first, the doctor will extract the fetal body through the cervix, collapse the skull, and remove the fetus through the cervix. This procedure is commonly referred to as "dilation and extraction" or "D & X" by the medical community.[72] The procedural similarities between the intact D & E and D & X procedures and the D & E procedure have prompted concern that the language of state partial-birth abortion bans may prohibit both methods of abortion.[73]

For the remainder of this chapter, the term "D & X" is used to represent both the intact D & E procedure and the D & X procedure.

In *Stenberg*, a Nebraska physician who performs abortions at a specialized abortion facility sought a declaration that Nebraska's partial-birth abortion ban statute violates the U.S. Constitution. The Nebraska statute provides:

> No partial birth abortion shall be performed in this state, unless such procedure is necessary to save the life of the mother whose life is endangered by a physical disorder, physical illness, or physical injury, including a life-endangering physical condition caused by or arising from the pregnancy itself.[74]

The term "partial birth abortion" is defined by the statute as "an abortion procedure in which the person performing the abortion partially delivers vaginally a living unborn child before killing the unborn child and completing the delivery."[75] The term "partially delivers vaginally a living unborn child before killing the unborn child" is further defined as "deliberately and intentionally delivering into the vagina a living unborn child, or a substantial portion thereof, for the purpose of performing a procedure that the person performing such procedure knows will kill the unborn child and does kill the unborn child."[76] Violation of the statute carries a prison term of up to 20 years and a fine of up to $25,000. In addition, a doctor who violates the statute is subject to the automatic revocation of his license to practice medicine in Nebraska.

Among his arguments, Dr. Carhart maintained that the meaning of the term "substantial portion" in the Nebraska statute is unclear and thus, could include the common D & E procedure in its ban of partial-birth abortions. Because the Nebraska legislature failed to provide a definition for "substantial portion," the U.S. Court of Appeals for the Eighth Circuit interpreted the Nebraska statute to proscribe both the D & X and D & E procedures: "if 'substantial portion' means an arm or a leg - and surely it must - then the ban ... encompasses both the D & E and the D & X procedures."[77] The Eighth

Circuit acknowledged that during the D & E procedure, the physician often inserts his forceps into the uterus, grasps a part of the living fetus, and pulls that part of the fetus into the vagina. Because the arm or leg is the most common part to be retrieved, the physician would violate the statute.[78]

The state argued that the statute's scienter or knowledge requirement limited its scope and made it applicable only to the D & X procedure. According to the state, the statute applied only to the deliberate and intentional performance of a partial birth abortion; that is, the partial delivery of a living fetus vaginally, the killing of the fetus, and the completion of the delivery.[79] However, the Eighth Circuit found that the D & E procedure involves all of the same steps: "The physician intentionally brings a substantial part of the fetus into the vagina, dismembers the fetus, leading to fetal demise, and completes the delivery. A physician need not set out with the intent to perform a D & X procedure in order to violate the statute."[80]

The Supreme Court affirmed the Eighth Circuit's decision by a 5-4 margin. The Court based its decision on two determinations. First, the Court concluded that the Nebraska statute lacks any exception for the preservation of the health of the mother. Second, the Court found that the statute imposes an undue burden on the right to choose abortion because its language covers more than the D & X procedure.

Despite the Court's previous instructions in *Roe* and *Casey*, that abortion regulation must include an exception where it is "necessary, in appropriate medical judgment, for the preservation of the life or health of the mother," the state argued that Nebraska's partial-birth abortion statute does not require a health exception because safe alternatives remains available to women and a ban on partial-birth abortions would create no risk to the health of women.[81] Although the Court conceded that the actual need for the D & X procedure is uncertain, it recognized that the procedure could be safer in certain circumstances.[82] Thus, the Court stated, "a statute that altogether forbids D & X creates a significant health risk ... [t]he statute consequently must contain a health exception."[83]

In its discussion of the undue burden that would be imposed if the Nebraska statute was upheld, the Court maintained that the plain language of the statute covers both the D & X and D & E procedures.[84] Although the Nebraska State Attorney General offered an interpretation of the statute that differentiated between the two procedures, the Court was reluctant to recognize such a view. Because the Court traditionally follows lower federal court interpretations of state law and because the Attorney General's interpretative views would not bind state courts, the Court held that the statute's reference to the delivery of "a living unborn child, or a substantial portion thereof" implicates both the D & X and D & E procedures.[85]

Because the *Stenberg* Court was divided by only one member, Justice O'Connor's concurrence raised concern among those who support a woman's right to choose. Justice O'Connor's concurrence indicated that a state statute prohibiting partial-birth abortions would likely withstand a constitutional challenge if it included an exception for situations where the health of the mother is at issue, and if it is "narrowly tailored to proscribing the D & X procedure alone."[86]

Justice O'Connor identified Kansas, Utah, and Montana as having partial-birth abortion statutes that differentiate appropriately between D & X and the other procedures.[87]

In April 2007, the Court again addressed the validity of a statute that prohibits the performance of partial-birth abortions. The federal Partial-Birth Abortion Ban Act of 2003 was signed by the President on November 5, 2003 (P.L. 108-105). In general, the act prohibits physicians from performing a partial-birth abortion except when it is necessary to save the life of a mother whose life is endangered by a physical disorder, physical illness, or physical injury, including a lifeendangering physical condition caused by or arising from the pregnancy itself. Physicians who violate the act are subject to a fine, imprisonment for not more than two years, or both.

In *Gonzales v. Carhart*, the Court upheld the federal statute, finding that, as a facial matter, it is not unconstitutionally vague and does not impose an undue burden on a woman's right to terminate her pregnancy.[88] The Court distinguished the federal statute from the Nebraska law at issue in *Stenberg*. According to the Court, the federal statute is not unconstitutionally vague because it provides doctors with a reasonable opportunity to know what conduct is prohibited.[89] Unlike the Nebraska law, which prohibited the delivery of a "substantial portion" of the fetus, the federal statute includes "anatomical landmarks" that identify when an abortion procedure will be subject to the act's prohibitions. The Court noted: "[I]f an abortion procedure does not involve the delivery of a living fetus to one of these 'anatomical landmarks'—where, depending on the presentation, either the fetal head or the fetal trunk past the navel is outside the body of the mother—the prohibitions of the act do not apply."[90]

The Court also maintained that the inclusion of a scienter or knowledge requirement in the federal statute alleviates any vagueness concerns. Because the act applies only when a doctor "deliberately and intentionally" delivers the fetus to an anatomical landmark, the Court concluded that a doctor performing the D & E procedure would not face criminal liability if a fetus is delivered beyond the prohibited points by mistake.[91] The Court observed: "The scienter requirements narrow the scope of the act's prohibition and limit prosecutorial discretion."[92]

In reaching its conclusion that the Partial-Birth Abortion Ban Act of 2003 does not impose an undue burden on a woman's right to terminate her pregnancy, the Court considered whether the federal statute is overbroad, prohibiting both the D & X and D & E procedures. The Court also considered the statute's lack of a health exception.

Relying on the plain language of the act, the Court determined that the federal statute could not be interpreted to encompass the D & E procedure. The Court maintained that the D & E procedure involves the removal of the fetus in pieces. In contrast, the federal statute uses the phrase "delivers a living fetus."[93] The Court stated: "D&E does not involve the delivery of a fetus because it requires the removal of fetal parts that are ripped from the fetus as they are pulled through the cervix."[94] The Court also identified the act's specific requirement of an "overt act" that kills the fetus as evidence of its inapplicability to the D & E procedure. The Court indicated: "This distinction matters because, unlike [D & X], standard D&E does not involve a delivery followed by a fatal act."[95] Because the act was found not to prohibit the D & E procedure, the Court concluded that it is not overbroad and does not impose an undue burden a woman's ability to terminate her pregnancy.

According to the Court, the absence of a health exception also did not result in an undue burden. Citing its decision in *Ayotte v. Planned Parenthood of Northern New England*,[96] the Court noted that a health exception would be required if it subjected women to significant health risks.[97] However, acknowledging medical disagreement about the act's requirements ever imposing significant health risks on women, the Court maintained that "the question becomes whether the act can stand when this medical uncertainty persists."[98] Reviewing its past decisions, the Court indicated that it has given state and federal legislatures wide discretion to pass legislation in areas where there is medical and scientific uncertainty.[99] The Court concluded that this medical uncertainty provides a sufficient basis to conclude in a facial challenge of the statute that it does not impose an undue burden.[100]

Although the Court upheld the Partial-Birth Abortion Ban Act of 2003 without a health exception, it acknowledged that there may be "discrete and well-defined instances" where the prohibited procedure "must be used."[101] However, the Court indicated that exceptions to the act should be considered in as-applied challenges brought by individual plaintiffs: "In an as-applied challenge the nature of the medical risk can be better quantified and balanced than in a facial attack."[102]

Justice Ginsburg authored the dissent in *Gonzales*. She was joined by Justices Stevens, Souter, and Breyer. Describing the Court's decision as "alarming," Justice Ginsburg questioned upholding the federal statute when the relevant procedure has been found to be appropriate in certain cases.[103] Citing expert testimony that had been introduced, Justice Ginsburg maintained that the prohibited procedure has safety advantages for women with certain medical conditions, including bleeding disorders and heart disease.[104]

Justice Ginsburg also criticized the Court's decision to uphold the statute without a health exception. Justice Ginsburg declared: "Not only does it defy the Court's longstanding precedent affirming the necessity of a health exception, with no carve-out for circumstances of medical uncertainty ... it gives short shrift to the records before us, carefully canvassed by the District Courts."[105] Moreover, according to Justice Ginsburg, the refusal to invalidate the Partial-Birth Abortion Ban Act of 2003 on facial grounds was "perplexing" in light of the Court's decision in *Stenberg*.[106] Justice Ginsburg noted: "[I]n materially identical circumstances we held that a statute lacking a health exception was unconstitutional on its face."[107]

Finally, Justice Ginsburg contended that the Court's decision "cannot be understood as anything more than an effort to chip away at a right declared again and again by [the] Court—and with increasing comprehension of its centrality to women's lives."[108] Citing the language used by the Court, including the phrase "abortion doctor" to describe obstetrician-gynecologists and surgeons who perform abortions, Justice Ginsburg maintained that "[t]he Court's hostility to the right *Roe* and *Casey* secured is not concealed."[109] She argued that when a statute burdens constitutional rights and the measure is simply a vehicle for expressing hostility to those rights, the burden is undue.[110]

End Notes

[1] 410 U.S. 113 (1973).
[2] 410 U.S. 179 (1973).
[3] *Webster v. Reproductive Health Services*, 492 U.S. 490 (1989); *Planned Parenthood of Southwestern Pennsylvania v. Casey*, 505 U.S. 833 (1992); *Carhart v. Gonzales*, 127 S. Ct. 1610 (2007).
[4] For additional discussion of the historical development of the regulation of abortion, *see Roe v. Wade*, 410 U.S. 113, 130-41. *See also* Eugene Quay, "Justifiable Abortion—Medical and Legal Foundations," 49 Geo. L.J. 173 (Winter 1960) and 49 Geo L.J. 395 (Spring 1961); James C. Mohr, Abortion in America (1978).

[5] 402 U.S. 62 (1971).

[6] *Roe*, 410 U.S. at 152.

[7] *Roe*, 410 U.S. at 152-3.

[8] *Roe*, 410 U.S. at 153.

[9] *Roe*, 410 U.S. at 148-50.

[10] *Roe*, 410 U.S. at 163.

[11] *Roe*, 410 U.S. at 163-4.

[12] *Id.*

[13] *Roe*, 410 U.S. at 160.

[14] *Roe*, 410 U.S. at 164-5.

[15] *Doe*, 410 U.S. at 196-9.

[16] *Doe*, 410 U.S. at 197-8.

[17] *Roe*, 410 U.S. at 157.

[18] *Roe*, 410 U.S. at 158.

[19] *Roe*, 410 U.S. at 160.

[20] *See Beal v. Doe*, 432 U.S. 438 (1977); *Maher v. Roe*, 432 U.S. 464 (1977); *Poelker v. Doe*, 432 U.S. 519 (1977) (*per curiam*).

[21] *See Harris v. McRae*, 448 U.S. 297 (1980).

[22] *See Williams v. Zbaraz*; *Miller v. Zbaraz*; *U.S. v. Zbaraz*, 448 U.S. 358 (1980).

[23] 428 U.S. 52 (1976).

[24] *See Freiman v. Ashcroft*, 584 F.2d 247, 251 (8th Cir. 1978), *aff'd mem.*, 440 U.S. 941 (1979).

[25] 462 U.S. 416 (1983).

[26] *City of Akron*, 462 U.S. at 442.

[27] *City of Akron*, 462 U.S. at 445.

[28] 376 F.Supp. 695 (S.D. Fla. 1974), *aff'd*, 428 U.S. 901 (1976).

[29] 443 U.S. 622 (1979).

[30] *City of Akron*, 462 U.S. at 439.

[31] *City of Akron*, 462 U.S. at 440.

[32] *City of Akron*, 462 U.S. at 441 (quoting *Bellotti*, 443 U.S. at 642 n.23.).

[33] 462 U.S. 476 (1983).

[34] 450 U.S. 398 (1981).

[35] *See Hartigan v. Zbaraz*, 484 U.S. 171 (1987).

[36] 497 U.S. 417 (1990).

[37] 497 U.S. 502 (1990).

[38] *Id.* at 511.

[39] *See Akron Center for Reproductive Health*, 497 U.S. at 510 ("[A]lthough our cases have required bypass procedures for parental consent statutes, we have not decided whether parental notice statutes must contains such procedures.").

[40] 520 U.S. 292 (1997).

[41] *See, e.g., Planned Parenthood, Sioux Falls Clinic v. Miller*, 63 F.3d 1452, 1460 (8th Cir. 1995) ("In short, parentalnotice provisions, like parental-consent provisions, are unconstitutional without a *Bellotti*-type bypass."); *Planned Parenthood of Blue Ridge v. Camblos*, 155 F.3d 352, 366 (4th Cir. 1998) ("[T]he question of whether a bypass is necessary within a parental notice (as opposed to consent) statute still remains open today.").

[42] *Danforth*, 428 U.S. at 80-1.

[43] *Ashcroft*, 462 U.S. at 487.

[44] *Ashcroft*, 462 U.S. at 490.

[45] 421 U.S. 809 (1975).

[46] 423 U.S. 9 (1975).

[47] *Menillo*, 423 U.S. at 9-11.

[48] *City of Akron*, 462 U.S. at 435.

[49] 462 U.S. 506 (1983).

[50] *Simopoulos*, 462 U.S. at 516.

[51] *Roe*, 410 U.S. at 160.

[52] *Roe*, 410 U.S. at 163.

[53] *Roe*, 410 U.S. at 160.

[54] *Danforth*, 428 U.S. at 64.

[55] *Id.*

[56] 439 U.S. 379 (1979).

[57] *Colautti*, 439 U.S. at 379, 397-401.

[58] *Ashcroft*, 462 U.S. at 486.

[59] *City of Akron*, 462 U.S. at 451.

[60] 476 U.S. 747 (1986).

[61] 492 U.S. 490 (1989).

[62] 500 U.S. 173 (1991).

[63] 505 U.S. 833 (1992).

[64] *Casey*, 505 U.S. at 856.

[65] *Casey*, 505 U.S. at 877.

[66] *Thornburgh v. American College of Obstetricians and Gynecologists*, 476 U.S. 747 (1986).

[67] *See Ada v. Guam Society of Obstetricians and Gynecologists*, 506 U.S. 1011 (1992); *Barnes v. Moore*, 506 U.S. 1021 (1992); *Barnes v. Mississippi,* 510 U.S. 976 (1993).

[68] 530 U.S. 914 (2000).

[69] *Stenberg*, 530 U.S. at 927.

[70] *Stenberg*, 530 U.S. at 924.

[71] *Stenberg*, 530 U.S. at 927.

[72] *Id.*

[73] *See Women's Medical Professional Corporation v. Voinovich*, 130 F.3d 187, 199 (6th Cir. 1997), cert. denied, 523 U.S. 1036 (1998) ("The primary distinction between the two procedures is that the D & E procedure results in a dismembered fetus while the D & X procedure results in a relatively intact fetus. More specifically, the D & E procedure involves dismembering the fetus in utero before compressing the skull by means of suction, while the D & X procedure involves removing intact all but the head of the fetus from the uterus and then compressing the skull by means of suction. In both procedures, the fetal head must be compressed, because it is usually too large to pass through a woman's dilated cervix. In the D & E procedure, this is typically accomplished by either suctioning the intracranial matter or by crushing the skull, while in the D & X procedure it is always accomplished by suctioning the intracranial matter.").

[74] Neb. Rev. Stat. § 28-328(1).

[75] Neb. Rev. Stat. § 28-326(9).

[76] *Id.*

[77] *Carhart v. Stenberg*, 192 F.3d 1142, 1150 (8th Cir. 1999).

[78] *Id.*

[79] *Carhart*, 192 F.3d at 1150.

[80] *Id.*

[81] *Stenberg*, 530 U.S. at 931 (quoting *Roe*, 410 U.S. at 164-65).

[82] *Stenberg*, 530 U.S. at 937.

[83] *Stenberg*, 530 U.S. at 938.

[84] *Stenberg*, 530 U.S. at 939.

[85] *Stenberg*, 530 U.S. at 940.

[86] *Stenberg*, 530 U.S. at 950. *See also Stenberg*, 530 U.S. at 951 ("If there were adequate alternative methods for a woman safely to obtain an abortion before viability, it is unlikely that prohibiting the D & X procedure alone would 'amount in practical terms to a substantial obstacle to a woman seeking an abortion' [*citation omitted*] ... Thus, a ban on partial-birth abortion that only proscribed the D & X method of abortion and that included an exception to preserve the life and health of the mother would be constitutional in my view.").

[87] *See Stenberg*, 530 U.S. at 950.

[88] 550 U.S. 124, 127 S. Ct. 1610 (2007). Unlike "as-applied" challenges, which consider the validity of a statute as applied to a particular plaintiff, facial challenges seek to invalidate a statute in all of its applications.

[89] *Gonzales*, 550 U.S. at __, 127 S. Ct. at 1628.

[90] *Gonzales*, 550 U.S. at __, 127 S. Ct. at 1627.

[91] *Gonzales*, 550 U.S. at __, 127 S. Ct. at 1628.

[92] *Gonzales*, 550 U.S. at __, 127 S. Ct. at 1629.

[93] 18 U.S.C. § 1531(b)(1)(A).

[94] *Gonzales*, 550 U.S. at __, 127 S. Ct. at 1630.

[95] *Gonzales*, 550 U.S. at __, 127 S. Ct. at 1631.

[96] 546 U.S. 320 (2006).

[97] *Gonzales*, 550 U.S. at __, 127 S. Ct. at 1635. For additional information on *Ayotte v. Planned Parenthood of Northern New England, see* CRS Report RL33467, *Abortion: Legislative Response*, by Jon O. Shimabukuro and Karen J. Lewis.

[98] *Gonzales*, 550 U.S. at __, 127 S. Ct. at 1636.

[99] *Id.*

[100] *Gonzales*, 550 U.S. at __, 127 S. Ct. at 1637. The Court indicated that its conclusion was also supported by other considerations, including the availability of the D&E procedure.

[101] *Gonzales*, 550 U.S. at __, 127 S. Ct. at 1638.

[102] *Gonzales*, 550 U.S. at __, 127 S. Ct. at 1638-39.

[103] *Gonzales*, 550 U.S. at __, 127 S. Ct. at 1641.

[104] *Gonzales*, 550 U.S. at __, 127 S. Ct. at 1644-45.

[105] *Gonzales*, 550 U.S. at __, 127 S. Ct. at 1646.

[106] *Gonzales*, 550 U.S. at __, 127 S. Ct. at 1650.

[107] *Id.*

[108] *Gonzales*, 550 U.S. at __, 127 S. Ct. at 1653.

[109] *Gonzales*, 550 U.S. at __, 127 S. Ct. at 1650.

[110] *Gonzales*, 550 U.S. at __, 127 S. Ct. at 1653.

In: Abortion: Legislative and Legal Issues   ISBN: 978-1-60741-522-0
Editor: Kevin G. Nolan   © 2010 Nova Science Publishers, Inc.

Chapter 2

ABORTION: LEGISLATIVE RESPONSE*

Jon O. Shimabukuro

SUMMARY

In 1973, the U.S. Supreme Court concluded in *Roe v. Wade* that the U.S. Constitution protects a woman's decision to terminate her pregnancy. In *Doe v. Bolton*, a companion decision, the Court found that a state may not unduly burden the exercise of that fundamental right with regulations that prohibit or substantially limit access to the means of effectuating the decision to have an abortion. Rather than settle the issue, the Court's rulings since *Roe* and *Doe* have continued to generate debate and have precipitated a variety of governmental actions at the national, state, and local levels designed either to nullify the rulings or limit their effect. These governmental regulations have, in turn, spawned further litigation in which resulting judicial refinements in the law have been no more successful in dampening the controversy.

In recent years, the rights enumerated in *Roe* have been redefined by decisions such as *Webster v. Reproductive Health Services*, which gave greater leeway to the States to restrict abortion, and *Rust v. Sullivan*, which narrowed the scope of permissible abortion-related activities that are linked to federal funding. The Court's decision in *Planned Parenthood of Southeastern Pennsylvania v. Casey*, which established the "undue burden" standard for

---

* This is an edited, reformatted and augmented version of a CRS Report for Congress publication, Report Rl33467, dated January 15, 2009.

determining whether abortion restrictions are permissible, gave Congress additional impetus to move on statutory responses to the abortion issue, such as the Freedom of Choice Act.

In each Congress since 1973, constitutional amendments to prohibit abortion have been introduced. These measures have been considered in committee, but none has been passed by either the House or the Senate.

Legislation to prohibit a specific abortion procedure, the so-called "partial-birth" abortion procedure, was passed in the 108th Congress. The Partial-Birth Abortion Ban Act appears to be one of the only examples of Congress restricting the performance of a medical procedure. Legislation that would prohibit the knowing transport of a minor across state lines for the purpose of obtaining an abortion has been introduced in numerous Congresses.

Since *Roe*, Congress has attached abortion funding restrictions to various appropriations measures. The greatest focus has been on restricting Medicaid abortions under the annual appropriations for the Department of Health and Human Services. This series of restrictions is popularly known as the "Hyde Amendments." Restrictions on the use of appropriated funds affect numerous federal entities, including the Department of Justice, where federal funds may not be used to perform abortions in the federal prison system except in cases of rape or endangerment of the mother. Such restrictions also have an impact in the District of Columbia, where both federal and local funds may not be used to perform abortions except in cases of rape, incest or where the mother is endangered, and affect international organizations like the United Nations Population Fund, which receives funds through the annual Foreign Operations appropriations measure.

MOST RECENT DEVELOPMENTS

On December 19, 2008, the Department of Health and Human Services (HHS) issued a new rule to implement existing federal health care conscience protection laws. Under the so-called Church Amendments, the Weldon Amendment, and certain provisions of the Public Health Service Act, specified individuals or entities may not be discriminated against for failing to participate in activities related to abortion.[1] The new rule provides definitions for some of the terms used in the conscience protection laws, establishes a written certification of compliance requirement for recipients of federal health care funds, and identifies HHS's Office of Civil Rights as the entity responsible for complaint handling and investigation.

HHS maintains that the new rule is necessary to educate the public and health care providers on the protections afforded by federal law.[2] The agency also notes that the new rule will "[foster] a more inclusive, tolerant environment in the health care industry than may currently exist."[3] Opponents of the new rule, however, contend that the new rule could jeopardize the health of individuals by making it more difficult to obtain health care services and information. They argue, for example, that the new rule could limit the availability of oral contraceptives.

Legislation that would appear to have halted the new rule was introduced in the 110th Congress. The Protecting Patients and Health Care Act (S. 20/H.R. 7310) was introduced by Senator Hillary Rodham Clinton and Representative Diana DeGette, but was not considered by either chamber. The 111th Congress may attempt to address the new rule pursuant to the Congressional Review Act, which permits the use of expedited procedures to disapprove an agency's final rule.[4] Alternately, Congress could enact legislation that amends the conscience protection laws to establish new definitions and procedures. Such legislation would have the likely effect of overriding the new rule. The rule could also be amended or rescinded by further administrative action. Such action, however, would have to follow procedures established by the Administrative Procedure Act.[5]

JUDICIAL HISTORY

The primary focus of this chapter is legislative action with respect to abortion. However, discussion of the various legislative proposals necessarily involves a brief discussion of the leading U.S. Supreme Court decisions concerning a woman's right to choose whether to terminate her pregnancy.[6]

Roe v. Wade and *Doe v. Bolton*

In 1973, the Supreme Court issued its landmark abortion rulings in *Roe v. Wade*, 410 U.S. 113 (1973), and *Doe v. Bolton*, 410 U.S. 179 (1973). In those cases, the Court found that Texas and Georgia statutes regulating abortion interfered to an unconstitutional extent with a woman's right to decide whether to terminate her pregnancy. The Texas statute forbade all abortions not necessary "for the purpose of saving the life of the mother." The Georgia enactment permitted abortions when continued pregnancy seriously threatened the woman's life or health, when the fetus was very likely to have severe birth defects, or when the pregnancy resulted from rape. The Georgia statute required, however, that abortions be performed only at accredited hospitals and only after approval by a hospital committee and two consulting physicians.

The Court's decisions were delivered by Justice Blackmun for himself and six other Justices. Justices White and Rehnquist dissented. The Court ruled that states may not categorically proscribe abortions by making their performance a crime, and that states may not make abortions unnecessarily difficult to obtain by prescribing elaborate procedural guidelines. The constitutional basis for the decisions rested upon the conclusion that the Fourteenth Amendment right of personal privacy embraced a woman's decision whether to carry a pregnancy to term. With regard to the scope of that privacy right, the Court stated that it included "only personal rights that can be deemed 'fundamental' or 'implicit in the concept of ordered liberty'" and "bears some extension to activities related to marriage, procreation, contraception, family relationship, and child rearing and education." *Roe*, 410 U.S. at 152-53. Such a right, the Court concluded, "is broad enough to encompass a woman's decision whether or not to terminate her pregnancy." *Id*. at 153.

With respect to protection of the right against state interference, the Court held that since the right of personal privacy is a fundamental right, only a "compelling State interest" could justify its limitation by a state. Thus, while it recognized the legitimacy of the state interest in protecting maternal health and the preservation of the fetus' potential life (*id*. at 148-150), as well as the existence of a rational connection between these two interests and the state's anti-abortion law, the Court held these interests insufficient to justify an absolute ban on abortions.

Instead, the Court emphasized the durational nature of pregnancy and found the state's interests to be sufficiently compelling to permit curtailment or prohibition of abortion only during specified stages of pregnancy. The High Court concluded that until the end of the first trimester, an abortion is no more dangerous to maternal health than childbirth itself, and found that "[With] respect to the State's important and legitimate interest in the health of the mother, the "compelling" point, in light of present medical knowledge, is at approximately the end of the first trimester." *Id*. at 163. Only after the first trimester does the state's interest in protecting maternal health provide a sufficient basis to justify state regulation of abortion, and then only to protect this interest. *Id*. at 163-64.

The "compelling" point with respect to the state's interest in the potential life of the fetus "is at viability." Following viability, the state's interest permits it to regulate and even proscribe an abortion except when necessary, in appropriate medical judgment, for the preservation of the life or health of the woman. *Id.* at 160. In summary, the Court's holding was grounded in this trimester framework analysis and the concept of fetal viability which was defined in post-natal terms. *Id.* at 164-65.

In *Doe v. Bolton*, 410 U.S. 179 (1973), the Court extended *Roe* by warning that just as states may not prevent abortion by making the performance a crime, states may not make abortions unreasonably difficult to obtain by prescribing elaborate procedural barriers. In *Doe*, the Court struck down state requirements that abortions be performed in licensed hospitals; that abortions be approved beforehand by a hospital committee; and that two physicians concur in the abortion decision. *Id.* at 196-99. The Court appeared to note, however, that this would not apply to a statute that protected the religious or moral beliefs of denominational hospitals and their employees. *Id.* at 197-98.

The Court in *Roe* also dealt with the question whether a fetus is a person under the Fourteenth Amendment and other provisions of the Constitution. The Court indicated that the Constitution never specifically defines "person", but added that in nearly all the sections where the word person appears, "the use of the word is such that it has application only post-natally. None indicates, with any assurance, that it has any possible pre-natal application." 410 U.S. at 157. The Court emphasized that, given the fact that in the major part of the 19th century prevailing legal abortion practices were far freer than today, the Court was persuaded "that the word 'person', as used in the Fourteenth Amendment, does not include the unborn." *Id.* at 158.

The Court did not, however, resolve the question of when life actually begins. While noting the divergence of thinking on this issue, it instead articulated the legal concept of "viability", defined as the point at which the fetus is potentially able to live outside the womb, although the fetus may require artificial aid. *Id.* at 160. Many other questions were also not addressed in *Roe* and *Doe*, but instead led to a wealth of post-*Roe* litigation.

Supreme Court Decisions Subsequent to *Roe* and *Doe*

The post-*Roe* litigation included challenges to state restrictions requiring informed consent/waiting periods (*Planned Parenthood v. Danforth*, 428 U.S.

52 (1976), *City of Akron v. Akron Center for Reproductive Health, Inc.*, 462 U.S. 416 (1983)); spousal/parental consent (*Planned Parenthood v. Danforth, supra, Bellotti v. Baird*, 443 U.S. 622 (1979), *City of Akron, supra, Planned Parenthood Association of Kansas City, Missouri Inc. v. Ashcroft*, 462 U.S. 476 (1983)); parental notice (*Bellotti v. Baird, supra, H. L. v. Matheson*, 450 U.S. 398 (1981), *Hartigan v. Zbaraz*, 484 U.S. 171 (1987), *Hodgson v. Minnesota*, 497 U.S. 417 (1990), *Ohio v. Akron Center for Reproductive Health*, 497 U.S. 502 (1990); reporting requirements (*Planned Parenthood v. Danforth, supra, Planned Parenthood of Kansas City, Missouri, Inc. v. Ashcroft, supra*); advertisement of abortion services (*Bigelow v. Virginia*, 421 U.S. 809 (1975); abortions by nonphysicians (*Connecticut v. Menillo*, 423 U.S. 9 (1975); locus of abortions (*City of Akron, supra*, Ashcroft, *supra, Simopoulos v. Virginia*, 462 U.S. 506 (1983)); viability, fetal testing, and disposal of fetal remains (*Planned Parenthood of Central Missouri v. Danforth, supra, Colautti v. Franklin*, 439 U.S. 379 (1979), *Ashcroft, supra, City of Akron, supra*); and "partial-birth" abortions (*Stenberg v. Carhart*, 530 U.S. 914 (2000)).

The Court in *Rust v. Sullivan*, 500 U.S. 173 (1991), upheld on both statutory and constitutional grounds HHS' Title X regulations restricting recipients of federal family planning funding from using federal funds to counsel women about the option of abortion. While *Rust* is probably better understood as a case involving First Amendment free speech rights rather than as a challenge to the constitutionally guaranteed substantive right to abortion, the Court, following its earlier public funding cases (*Maher v. Roe* and *Harris v. McRae*), did conclude that a woman's right to an abortion was not burdened by the Title X regulations. The Court reasoned that there was no constitutional violation because the government has no duty to subsidize an activity simply because it is constitutionally protected and because a woman is "in no worse position than if Congress had never enacted Title X."

In addition to *Rust*, the Court decided several other noteworthy cases involving abortion following *Roe*. *Webster v. Reproductive Health Services*, 492 U.S. 490 (1989), and *Planned Parenthood of Southeastern Pennsylvania v. Casey*, 505 U.S. 833 (1992), illustrate a shift in direction by the Court from the type of constitutional analysis it articulated in *Roe*. These cases and other more recent cases, such as *Stenberg v. Carhart*, 530 U.S. 914 (2000), and *Ayotte v. Planned Parenthood of Northern New England*, 126 S.Ct. 961 (2006), have implications for future legislative action and how enactments will be judged by the courts in the years to come. *Webster, Casey*, and *Ayotte* are

unconstitutional applications of a statute while leaving other
force ... or to sever its problematic portions while leaving the
t." *Id*. at 328-29.

identified three interrelated principles that inform its approach
irst, the Court tries not to nullify more of a legislature's work
ry because a ruling of unconstitutionality frustrates the intent of
resentatives of the people.

he Court restrains itself from rewriting a state law to conform to
requirements, even as it attempts to salvage the law. The Court
at its constitutional mandate and institutional competence are
ng that "making distinctions in a murky constitutional context"
a far more serious invasion of the legislative domain than the
to take. *Id*. at 330.

he touchstone for any decision about remedy is legislative intent;
urt cannot use its remedial powers to circumvent the intent of the
The Court observed that "[a]fter finding an application or portion
e unconstitutional, we must next ask: Would the legislature have
what is left of its statute to no statute at all?" *Id*.

mand, the lower courts were expected to determine the intent of the
pshire legislature when it enacted the parental notification statute.
the State argued that the measure's severability clause illustrated the
e's understanding that the act should continue in force even if certain
ns were invalidated, the respondents insisted that New Hampshire
rs actually preferred no statute rather than one that would be enjoined
anner described by the Court. On February 1, 2007, a federal district
New Hampshire entered a procedural order that stayed consideration
ase while a bill to repeal the Parental Notification Prior to Abortion Act
nding in the state legislature.[7] The act was subsequently repealed by the
ture, effective June 29, 2007.

ome criticized the Court's willingness to invalidate the New Hampshire
only as it applied during medical emergencies. While it is not
mmon for federal courts to save a statute from invalidation by severing
nstitutional provisions, these courts have generally limited this practice to
ral statutes. Critics maintained that the Court's opinion represented an
ermissible expansion of federal judicial power over the states. They also
ued that the opinion could encourage states to enact legislation with
visions that are possibly or clearly unconstitutional, knowing that a
iewing court will sever the impermissible provisions and allow the
aining statute to continue in force.

discussed in the subsequent sections of this chapter. A discussion of *Stenberg* is included in the "Partial-Birth Abortion" section of the report.

Webster

The Supreme Court upheld the constitutionality of the State of Missouri's abortion statute in *Webster v. Reproductive Health Services*, 492 U.S. 49 (1989). In this 5-4 decision, while the majority did not overrule *Roe*, it indicated that it was willing to apply a less stringent standard of review to state restrictions on abortion. *Webster* made it clear that state legislatures have considerable discretion to pass restrictive legislation in the future, with the likelihood that such laws would probably pass constitutional muster.

The main provisions in the 1986 Missouri law upheld by the Court included (1) barring public employees from performing or assisting in abortions not necessary to save the life of the mother; (2) barring the use of public buildings for performing abortions, despite the fact that there were no public monies involved (e.g., a building situated on public land); and (3) requiring physicians believing a woman desiring an abortion to be at least 20 weeks pregnant to perform tests to determine whether the fetus is viable. The *Webster* ruling was narrow in that it did not affect private doctors' offices or clinics, where most abortions are performed. Its significance derives more from the rationales articulated by the five justices regarding how abortion restrictions would be reviewed in the future. However, because the Missouri law did not limit abortion prior to viability, the plurality did not believe it was necessary to consider overruling *Roe*. *Webster* set the stage for the Court's 1992 decision in *Casey* where a real shift in direction was pronounced.

Casey

Both *Webster* and *Rust* energized legislative activity, the former at both the federal and state levels and the latter at the federal level. Some of the state legislative proposals that became law were challenged in the courts (e.g., Pennsylvania, Guam, Louisiana, and Utah). The Pennsylvania case, *Planned Parenthood of Southeastern Pennsylvania v. Casey*, 505 U.S. 833 (1992), was decided by the Supreme Court on June 29, 1992. In a highly fractionated 5-4 decision, the Court reaffirmed the basic constitutional right to an abortion while simultaneously allowing some new restrictions. Justices O'Connor,

Kennedy, and Souter wrote the plurality opinion, and they were joined in part by Justices Stevens and Blackmun. Chief Justice Rehnquist and Justices White, Scalia, and Thomas dissented. The Court refused to overrule *Roe*, and the plurality explained at length why it was important to follow precedent. At the same time, the plurality indicated that state laws which contained an outright ban on abortion would be unconstitutional. Nevertheless, the Court abandoned the trimester framework articulated in *Roe* and the strict scrutiny standard of judicial review of abortion restrictions. Instead, it adopted a new analysis, "undue burden."

Courts will now need to ask the question whether a state abortion restriction has the effect of imposing an "undue burden" on a woman's right to obtain an abortion. "Undue burden" was defined as a "substantial obstacle in the path of a woman seeking an abortion of a nonviable fetus." 505 U.S. at 877.

The Court applied this new analysis to the Pennsylvania statute and concluded that four of the provisions did not impose an undue burden on the right to abortion and were constitutional. The provisions that were upheld involved the 24-hour waiting period; informed consent; parental consent for minors' abortions with a judicial bypass; and reporting requirements. The spousal notification provision, which required a married woman to tell her husband if she intended to have an abortion, did not survive the "undue burden" test and was struck down as unconstitutional.

The Court's decision in *Casey* was significant because the new standard of review appeared to allow more state restrictions to pass constitutional muster. In addition, the *Casey* Court found that the state's interest in protecting the potentiality of human life extended throughout the course of the pregnancy. Thus, the state could regulate, even to the point of favoring childbirth over abortion, from the outset. Under *Roe*, which utilized the trimester framework, a woman's decision to terminate her pregnancy was reached in consultation with her doctor with virtually no state involvement during the first trimester of pregnancy.

Moreover, under *Roe*, abortion was a "fundamental right" that could not be restricted by the state except to serve a "compelling" state interest. *Roe*'s strict scrutiny form of review resulted in most state regulations being invalidated during the first two trimesters of pregnancy. The "undue burden" standard allowed greater regulation during that period. This is evident from the fact that the *Casey* Court overruled, in part, two of its earlier decisions which had followed *Roe*: *City of Akron v. Akron Center of Reproductive Health*, 462 U.S. 416 (1983), and *Thornburgh v. American College of Obstetricians and*

Gynecologists, 476 U.S. 747 (1986). scrutiny, struck down 24-hour w provisions; whereas in *Casey*, applyin upheld similar provisions.

Casey had its greatest immediate Pennsylvania; however, its reasoning restrictions that could withstand challeng

Ayotte

In *Ayotte v. Planned Parenthood of Nor* (2006), the Court concluded that a wholesale Parental Notification Prior to Abortion Act only a few applications of the act raised cor remanded the case to the lower courts to rei injunctive relief.

The New Hampshire law at issue in *Ayott* performing an abortion on a pregnant minor or a or conservator was appointed until 48 hours after to at least one parent or guardian. The notifica waived under certain specified circumstances. For not required if the attending abortion provider cert necessary to prevent the woman's death and there provide the required notice.

Planned Parenthood of Northern New England an providers challenged the New Hampshire statute on the include an explicit waiver that would allow an abortic protect the health of the woman. The First Circuit invali entirety on that basis. The First Circuit also maintaine exception was impermissibly vague and forced physicians patients' lives by preventing them from performing a notification until they were certain that death was imminent

Declining to revisit its prior abortion decisions, the *Ayotte* presented a question of remedy. Maintaining that unconstitutional only in medical emergencies, the Court d more narrow remedy, rather than the wholesale invalidation appropriate: "Generally speaking, when confronting a constitu statute, we try to limit the solution to the problem. We prefer, i

Public Funding of Abortions

After the Supreme Court's decisions in *Roe* and *Doe*, one of the first federal legislative responses was the enactment of restrictions on the use of federal money for abortions (e.g., restrictions on Medicaid funds—the so-called Hyde Amendment). Almost immediately, these restrictions were challenged in the courts. Two categories of public funding cases have been heard and decided by the Supreme Court: those involving (1) funding restrictions for nontherapeutic (elective) abortions; and (2) funding limitations for therapeutic (medically necessary) abortions.

The 1977 Trilogy—Restrictions on Public Funding of Nontherapeutic or Elective Abortions

The Supreme Court, in three related decisions, ruled that the states have neither a statutory nor a constitutional obligation to fund elective abortions or provide access to public facilities for such abortions (*Beal v. Doe*, 432 U.S. 438 (1977); *Maher v. Roe*, 432 U.S. 464 (1977); and *Poelker v. Doe*, 432 U.S. 519 (1977) (per curiam)).

In *Beal v. Doe*, the Court held that nothing in the language or legislative history of Title XIX of the Social Security Act (Medicaid) requires a participating state to fund every medical procedure falling within the delineated categories of medical care. The Court ruled that it was not inconsistent with the act's goals to refuse to fund unnecessary medical services. However, the Court did indicate that Title XIX left a state free to include coverage for nontherapeutic abortions should it choose to do so. Similarly, in *Maher v. Roe*, the Court held that the Equal Protection Clause does not require a state participating in the Medicaid program to pay expenses incident to nontherapeutic abortions simply because the state has made a policy choice to pay expenses incident to childbirth. More particularly, Connecticut's policy of favoring childbirth over abortion was held not to impinge upon the fundamental right of privacy recognized in *Roe*, which protects a woman from undue interference in her decision to terminate a pregnancy. Finally, in *Poelker v. Doe*, the Court upheld a municipal regulation that denied indigent pregnant women nontherapeutic abortions at public hospitals. It also held that staffing those hospitals with personnel opposed to the performance of abortions did not violate the Equal Protection Clause of the Constitution. *Poelker*, however, did not deal with the question of private hospitals and their authority to prohibit abortion services.

Public Funding of Therapeutic or Medically Necessary Abortions

The 1977 Supreme Court decisions left open the question whether federal law, such as the Hyde Amendment (restrictions on Medicaid funding of abortion), or similar state laws, could validly prohibit governmental funding of therapeutic abortions.

The Court in *Harris v. McRae*, 448 U.S. 297 (1980), ruled 5-4 that the Hyde Amendment's abortion funding restrictions were constitutional. The majority found that the Hyde Amendment neither violated the due process or equal protection guarantees of the Fifth Amendment nor the Establishment [of religion] Clause of the First Amendment. The Court also upheld the right of a state participating in the Medicaid program to fund only those medically necessary abortions for which it received federal reimbursement. In companion cases raising similar issues, the Court held that an Illinois statutory funding restriction comparable to the federal Hyde Amendment also did not contravene the constitutional restrictions of the Equal Protection Clause of the Fourteenth Amendment (*Williams v. Zbaraz*; *Miller v. Zbaraz*; *U.S. v. Zbaraz*, 448 U.S. 358 (1980)). The Court's rulings in *McRae* and *Zbaraz* mean there is no statutory or constitutional obligation of the states or the federal government to fund medically necessary abortions.

Partial-Birth Abortion

On June 28, 2000, the Court decided *Stenberg v. Carhart*, 530 U.S. 914 (2000), its first substantive abortion case since *Casey*. In *Stenberg*, the Court determined that a Nebraska statute that prohibited the performance of so-called "partial-birth" abortions was unconstitutional because it failed to include an exception to protect the health of the mother and because the language defining the prohibited procedure was too vague.[8] In affirming the decision of the Eighth Circuit, the Court agreed that the language of the Nebraska statute could be interpreted to prohibit not just the dilation and extraction (D&X) procedure that pro-life advocates oppose, but the standard dilation and evacuation (D&E) procedure that is the most common abortion procedure during the second trimester of pregnancy. The Court believed that the statute was likely to prompt those who perform the D&E procedure to stop because of fear of prosecution and conviction. The result would be the imposition of an "undue burden" on a woman's ability to have an abortion.

During the 106th Congress, both the Senate and House passed bills that would have prohibited the performance of partial-birth abortions. The Senate passed the Partial-Birth Abortion Ban Act of 1999 (S. 1692) on October 21, 1999 by a vote of 63-34. H.R. 3660, the Partial-Birth Abortion Ban Act of 2000, was passed by the House on April 5, 2000 by a vote of 287-141. Although the House requested a conference, no further action was taken. Similar partial-birth abortion measures were vetoed during the 104th and 105th Congresses. In both instances, President William J. Clinton focused on the failure to include an exception to the ban when the mother's health is an issue.

During the 107th Congress, the House passed H.R. 4965, the Partial-Birth Abortion Ban Act of 2002, by a vote of 274-151. H.R. 4965 would have prohibited physicians from performing a partial-birth abortion except when it was necessary to save the life of a mother whose life was endangered by a physical disorder, physical illness, or physical injury, including a lifeendangering physical condition caused by or arising from the pregnancy itself. The bill defined the term "partial-birth abortion" to mean an abortion in which "the person performing the abortion deliberately and intentionally vaginally delivers a living fetus until, in the case of a headfirst presentation, the entire fetal head is outside the body of the mother, or, in the case of breech presentation, any part of the fetal trunk past the navel is outside the body of the mother for the purpose of performing an overt act that the person knows will kill the partially delivered living fetus." Physicians who violated the act would have been subject to a fine, imprisonment for not more than two years, or both. H.R. 4965 was not considered by the Senate.

During the 108th Congress, on November 5, 2003, the President signed S. 3, the Partial-Birth Abortion Ban Act of 2003 (P.L. 108-105). The Senate initially passed S. 3 on March 13, 2003 by a vote of 64-33. H.R. 760, a companion measure to S. 3, was passed by the House on June 4, 2003 by a vote of 282-139. Shortly after passage of H.R. 760, pursuant to H.Res. 257, the language of S. 3 was struck, and the provisions of H.R. 760 were inserted into the measure. On September 17, 2003, the Senate voted 93-0 to reject the House amendment to S. 3. The Senate's vote moved the two measures to conference. On September 30, 2003, a House-Senate conference committee agreed to report a version of the bill that was identical to the House-passed measure. The House approved H.Rept. 108-288, the conference report for the Partial-Birth Abortion Ban Act of 2003, by a vote of 281-142 on October 2, 2003. The Senate agreed to the conference report by a vote of 64-34 on October 21, 2003.

In general, the act prohibits physicians from performing a partial-birth abortion except when it is necessary to save the life of a mother whose life is endangered by a physical disorder, physical illness, or physical injury, including a life-endangering physical condition caused by or arising from the pregnancy itself. Physicians who violate the act are subject to a fine, imprisonment for not more than two years, or both.

Despite the Court's holding in *Stenberg* and past decisions that have found that restrictions on abortion must allow for the performance of an abortion when it is necessary to protect the health of the mother, the Partial-Birth Abortion Ban Act of 2003 does not include such an exception. In his introductory statement for the act, Senator Rick Santorum discussed the measure's lack of a health exception.[9] He maintained that an exception is not necessary because of the risks associated with partial-birth abortions. Senator Santorum insisted that congressional hearings and expert testimony demonstrate "that a partial birth abortion is never necessary to preserve the health of the mother, poses significant health risks to the woman, and is outside the standard of medical care."[10]

Within two days of the act's signing, federal courts in Nebraska, California, and New York blocked its enforcement. On April 18, 2007, the Court upheld the Partial-Birth Abortion Ban Act of 2003, finding that, as a facial matter, it is not unconstitutionally vague and does not impose an undue burden on a woman's right to terminate her pregnancy.[11] In *Gonzales v. Carhart*, 127 S.Ct. 1610 (2007), the Court distinguished the federal statute from the Nebraska law at issue in *Stenberg*. According to the Court, the federal statute is not unconstitutionally vague because it provides doctors with a reasonable opportunity to know what conduct is prohibited. *Id*. at 1628. Unlike the Nebraska law, which prohibited the delivery of a "substantial portion" of the fetus, the federal statute includes "anatomical landmarks" that identify when an abortion procedure will be ubject to the act's prohibitions. The Court noted: "[I]f an abortion procedure does not involve the delivery of a living fetus to one of these 'anatomical landmarks'—where, depending on the presentation, either the fetal head or the fetal trunk past the navel is outside the body of the mother—the prohibitions of the Act do not apply." *Id*. at 1627.

The Court also maintained that the inclusion of a scienter or knowledge requirement in the federal statute alleviates any vagueness concerns. Because the act applies only when a doctor "deliberately and intentionally" delivers the fetus to an anatomical landmark, the Court concluded that a doctor performing the D&E procedure would not face criminal liability if a fetus is delivered beyond the prohibited points by mistake. *Id*. at 1628. The Court observed: "The scienter requirements narrow the scope of the Act's prohibition and limit prosecutorial discretion." *Id*. at 1629.

In reaching its conclusion that the Partial-Birth Abortion Ban Act of 2003 does not impose an undue burden on a woman's right to terminate her pregnancy, the Court considered whether the federal statute is overbroad, prohibiting both the D&X and D&E procedures. The Court also considered the statute's lack of a health exception.

Relying on the plain language of the act, the Court determined that the federal statute could not be interpreted to encompass the D&E procedure. The Court maintained that the D&E procedure involves the removal of the fetus in pieces. In contrast, the federal statute uses the phrase "delivers a living fetus." The Court stated: "D&E does not involve the delivery of a fetus because it requires the removal of fetal parts that are ripped from the fetus as they are pulled through the cervix." *Id.* at 1630. The Court also identified the act's specific requirement of an "overt act" that kills the fetus as evidence of its inapplicability to the D&E procedure. The Court indicated: "This distinction matters because, unlike [D&X], standard D&E does not involve a delivery followed by a fatal act." *Id.* at 1631. Because the act was found not to prohibit the D&E procedure, the Court concluded that it is not overbroad and does not impose an undue burden a woman's ability to terminate her pregnancy.

According to the Court, the absence of a health exception also did not result in an undue burden. Citing its decision in *Ayotte*, the Court noted that a health exception would be required if the act subjected women to significant health risks. *Id.* at 1635. However, acknowledging medical disagreement about the act's requirements ever imposing significant health risks on women, the Court maintained that "the question becomes whether the Act can stand when this medical uncertainty persists." *Id.* at 1636. Reviewing its past decisions, the Court indicated that it has given state and federal legislatures wide discretion to pass legislation in areas where there is medical and scientific uncertainty. *Id.* The Court concluded that this medical uncertainty provides a sufficient basis to conclude in a facial challenge of the statute that it does not impose an undue burden. *Id.* at 1637.

Although the Court upheld the Partial-Birth Abortion Ban Act of 2003 without a health exception, it acknowledged that there may be "discrete and well-defined instances" where the prohibited procedure "must be used." *Id.* at 1638. However, the Court indicated that exceptions to the act should be considered in as-applied challenges brought by individual plaintiffs: "In an as-applied challenge the nature of the medical risk can be better quantified and balanced than in a facial attack." *Id.* at 1638-39.

Justice Ginsburg authored the dissent in *Gonzales*. She was joined by Justices Stevens, Souter, and Breyer. Describing the Court's decision as "alarming," Justice Ginsburg questioned upholding the federal statute when the relevant procedure has been found to be appropriate in certain cases. *Id.* at 1641. Citing expert testimony that had been introduced, Justice Ginsburg maintained that the prohibited procedure has safety advantages for women with certain medical conditions, including bleeding disorders and heart disease. *Id.* at 1644-45.

Justice Ginsburg also criticized the Court's decision to uphold the statute without a health exception. Justice Ginsburg declared: "Not only does it defy the Court's longstanding precedent affirming the necessity of a health exception, with no carve-out for circumstances of medical uncertainty ... it gives short shrift to the records before us, carefully canvassed by the District Courts." *Id.* at 1646. Moreover, according to Justice Ginsburg, the refusal to invalidate the Partial-Birth Abortion Ban Act of 2003 on facial grounds was "perplexing" in light of the Court's decision in *Stenberg. Id.* at 1650. Justice Ginsburg noted: "[I]n materially identical circumstances we held that a statute lacking a health exception was unconstitutional on its face." *Id.*

Finally, Justice Ginsburg contended that the Court's decision "cannot be understood as anything more than an effort to chip away at a right declared again and again by [the] Court—and with increasing comprehension of its centrality to women's lives." *Id.* at 1653. Citing the language used by the Court, including the phrase "abortion doctor" to describe obstetrician-gynecologists and surgeons who perform abortions, Justice Ginsburg maintained that "[t]he Court's hostility to the right *Roe* and *Casey* secured is not concealed." *Id.* at 1650. She argued that when a statute burdens constitutional rights and the measure is simply a vehicle for expressing hostility to those rights, the burden should be viewed as "undue." *Id.* at 1653.

LEGISLATIVE HISTORY

Rather than settle the issue, the Court's decisions in *Roe* and *Doe* have prompted debate and precipitated a variety of governmental actions at the national, state, and local levels to limit their effect. The 110th Congress continued to be a forum for proposed legislation and constitutional amendments aimed at limiting or prohibiting the practice of abortion. This section examines the history of the federal legislative response to the abortion issue.

In the decade prior to the decision in *Roe*, 10 pieces of legislation relating to abortion were introduced in either the House or the Senate. Since 1973, more than 1,000 separate legislative proposals have been introduced. The wide disparity in these statistics illustrates the impetus that the Court's 1973 decisions gave to congressional action. By far, most of these proposals have sought to restrict the availability of abortions. A few measures have been introduced to better secure the right to terminate a pregnancy. The Freedom of Choice Act (FOCA), for example, was introduced and debated in both the 102nd and 103rd Congresses, but was never enacted. FOCA attempts to codify *Roe* legislatively, and was reintroduced in the 110th Congress. The Freedom of Access to Clinic Entrances Act of 1994, P.L. 103-259 (18 U.S.C. 248), made it a federal crime to use force, or the threat of force, to intimidate abortion clinic workers or women seeking abortions.

Proponents of more restrictive abortion legislation have employed a variety of legislative initiatives to achieve this end, with varying degrees of success. Initially, legislators focused their efforts on the passage of a constitutional amendment which would overrule the Supreme Court's decision in *Roe*. This course, however, proved to be problematic.

Constitutional Amendments

Since 1973, a series of constitutional amendments have been introduced in each Congress in an attempt to overrule the Court's decision in *Roe*. To date, no constitutional amendment has been passed in either the House or the Senate. Indeed, for several years, proponents had difficulty getting the measures reported out of committee. Interest in the constitutional approach peaked in the 94th Congress when nearly 80 amendments were introduced. By the 98th Congress, the number had significantly declined. It was during this time that the Senate brought to the floor the only constitutional amendment on abortion that has ever been debated and voted on in either House.

During the 98th Congress, S.J.Res. 3 was introduced. Subcommittee hearings were held, and the full Judiciary Committee voted (9-9) to send the amendment to the Senate floor without recommendation. As reported, S.J.Res. 3 included a subcommittee amendment eliminating the enforcement language and declared simply, "A right to abortion is not secured by this Constitution." By adopting this proposal, the subcommittee established its intent to remove federal institutions from the policymaking process with respect to abortion and reinstate state authorities as the ultimate decisionmakers.

S.J.Res. 3 was considered in the Senate on June 27 and 28, 1983. The amendment required a twothirds vote to pass the Senate since super-majorities of both Houses of Congress must approve a constitutional amendment before it can be submitted to the states. On June 28, 1983, S.J.Res. 3 was defeated (50-49), not having obtained the two-thirds vote necessary for a constitutional amendment.[12]

Statutory Provisions

Bills that Seek to Prohibit the Right to Abortion by Statute

As an alternative to a constitutional amendment to prohibit or limit the practice of abortion, opponents of abortion have introduced a variety of bills designed to accomplish the same objective without resorting to the complex process of amending the Constitution. Authority for such action is said to emanate from Section 5 of the Fourteenth Amendment, which empowers the Congress to enforce the due process and equal protection guarantees of the amendment "by appropriate legislation." One such bill, S. 158, introduced during the 97th Congress, would have declared as a congressional finding of fact that human life begins at conception, and would, it was contended by its sponsors, allow states to enact laws protecting human life, including fetuses. Hearings on the bill were marked by controversy over the constitutionality of the declaration that human life begins at conception, which contradicted the Supreme Court's specific holding in *Roe*, and over the withdrawal of lower federal court jurisdiction over suits challenging state laws enacted pursuant to federal legislation. A modified version of S. 158 was approved in subcommittee, but that bill, S. 1741, had no further action in the 97th Congress.

Hyde-Type Amendments to Appropriation Bills

As an alternative to these unsuccessful attempts to prohibit abortion outright, opponents of abortion sought to ban the use of federal monies to pay for the performance of abortions. They focused their efforts primarily on the Medicaid program since the vast majority of federally funded abortions were reimbursed under Medicaid.

The Medicaid program was established in 1965 to fund medical care for indigent persons through a federal-state cost-sharing arrangement; however, abortions were not initially covered under the program. During the Nixon Administration, the Department of Health, Education and Welfare (HEW) decided to reimburse states for the funds used to provide abortions to poor women. This policy decision was influenced by the Supreme Court's decision in *Roe* which, in addition to decriminalizing abortion, was seen as legitimizing the status of abortion as a medical procedure for the purposes of the Medicaid program.

Since *Roe*, Congress has attached abortion funding restrictions to numerous appropriations bills. Although the Foreign Assistance Act of 1973, P.L. 93-189, was the first such enactment, the greatest focus has been on restricting Medicaid abortions under the annual appropriations for the Department of Health, Education, and Welfare (HEW) (now the Department of Health and Human Services).

The first of a series of restrictions, popularly referred to as the "Hyde Amendments," was attached to the FY1977 Departments of Labor and Health, Education, and Welfare Appropriation Act, P.L. 94-439. As originally offered by Representative Hyde, the proposal would have prohibited the funding of all abortions. A compromise amendment offered by Representative Conte was eventually agreed to, providing that "None of the funds contained in this act shall be used to perform abortions except where the life of the mother would be endangered if the fetus were carried to term."

In subsequent years, Hyde Amendments were sometimes reworded to include exceptions for rape and incest or long-lasting physical health damage to the mother. However, from the 97th Congress until recently the language has been identical to the original enactment, allowing only an exception to preserve the life of the mother. In 1993, during the first year of the Clinton Administration, coverage under the Hyde Amendment was expanded to again include cases of rape and incest. Efforts to restore the original language (providing for only the life of the woman exception) failed in the 104th Congress.

The Hyde Amendment process has not been limited to the Labor/HHS appropriation. Beginning with P.L. 95-457, the Department of Defense Appropriation Acts have contained Hyde-type abortion limitations. This recurring prohibition was eventually codified and made permanent by P.L. 98-525, the Department of Defense Authorization Act of 1984.

Beginning with P.L. 96-93, the District of Columbia (D.C.) Appropriations Acts have contained restrictive abortion provisions. In recent years there have been efforts to expand the prohibitions to District funds as well as the federal funds appropriated. The passage of P.L. 100-462, the FY1989 D.C. Appropriations Act, marked the first successful attempt to extend abortion restrictions to the use of District funds. In 1993 and 1994, lawmakers approved a prohibition that applied only to federal monies. The 104th Congress approved a ban on all government funding of abortion (federal and D.C.), except in cases of rape, incest or danger to a woman's life. This ban has continued in recent appropriations measures for the District.

In 1983, the Hyde Amendment process was extended to the Department of the Treasury and Postal Service Appropriations Act, prohibiting the use of Federal Employee Health Benefits to pay for abortions except when the life of the woman was in danger. Prior to this, it had been reported that in 1980, for instance, federal government health insurance plans paid an estimated $9 million for abortions, both therapeutic and non-therapeutic. The following year the Office of Personnel Management (OPM) attempted through administrative action to eliminate non-lifesaving abortion coverage. This action was challenged by federal employee unions, and the U.S. district court held that OPM acted outside the scope of its authority, and that absent a specific congressional statutory directive, there was no basis for OPM's decision. *American Federation of Government Employees v. AFL-CIO*, 525 F.Supp. 250 (1981). It was this background that led to the 1983 congressional action to include the prohibition on coverage for abortion in federal employee health insurance plans except when the life of the woman was in danger. This prohibition was removed in 1993. However, the 104th Congress passed language prohibiting the use of federal money for abortion under the Federal Employee Health Benefit Program except in cases where the life of the mother would be endangered or in cases of rape or incest.

Finally, under Department of Justice appropriations, funding of abortions in prisons is prohibited except where the life of the mother is endangered, or in cases of rape. First enacted as part of the FY1987 Continuing Resolution, P.L. 99-591, this provision has been reenacted as part of the annual spending bill in each subsequent fiscal year, but the language has been modified in recent years.

Other Legislation

In addition to the temporary funding limitations contained in appropriation bills, abortion restrictions of a more permanent nature have been enacted in a variety of contexts since 1970. For example, the Family Planning Services and Population Research Act of 1970, P.L. 91-572 (42 U.S.C. 300a-6), bars the use of funds for programs in which abortion is a method of family planning.

The Legal Services Corporation Act of 1974, P.L. 93-355 (42 U.S.C. 2996f(b)(8)), prohibits lawyers in federally funded legal aid programs from providing legal assistance for procuring nontherapeutic abortions and prohibits legal aid in proceedings to compel an individual or an institution to perform an abortion, assist in an abortion, or provide facilities for an abortion.

The Pregnancy Discrimination Act, P.L. 95-555 (42 U.S.C. 2000e(k)), provides that employers are not required to pay health insurance benefits for abortion except to save the life of the mother, but does not preclude employers from providing abortion benefits if they choose to do so.

The Civil Rights Restoration Act of 1988, P.L. 100-259 (20 U.S.C. 1688), states that nothing in the measure either prohibits or requires any person or entity from providing or paying for services related to abortion.

The Civil Rights Commission Amendments Act of 1994, P.L. 103-419 (42 U.S.C. 1975a(f)), prohibits the Commission from studying or collecting information about U.S. laws and policies concerning abortion.

LEGISLATION IN THE 110TH CONGRESS

Legislation that would have prohibited the knowing transport of a minor across state lines for the purpose of obtaining an abortion was again introduced in the 110th Congress. The Child Interstate Abortion Notification Act was introduced on February 15, 2007 by Representative Ileana Ros-Lehtinen. The measure would have required a physician who performed or induced an abortion on a minor who was a resident of a state other than the state in which the abortion was performed to provide at least 24 hours written notice to a parent of the minor before performing the abortion. A parent who suffered harm from a violation of the notice requirement could have obtained appropriate relief in a civil action. The notice requirement would not have applied in certain specified situations, including those where the abortion was necessary to save the life of the minor because her life was endangered by a physical disorder, physical injury, or physical illness.

Legislation that would have required an abortion provider or his agent to provide specified information to a pregnant woman prior to the performance of an abortion was also introduced. The Unborn Child Pain Awareness Act was introduced by Senator Sam Brownback in the Senate on January 22, 2007, (S. 356) and by Representative Christopher H. Smith in the House on August 3, 2007 (H.R. 3442). Under the measure, an abortion provider or his agent would have been required, prior to the performance of an abortion, to communicate specified information to the pregnant woman, provide an "Unborn Child Pain Awareness Brochure" to the woman, and obtain the woman's signature on an "Unborn Child Pain Awareness Decision Form."

The act's requirements would have applied only when an abortion was being performed on a socalled "pain-capable unborn child." The term "pain-capable unborn child" was defined by the act to mean "an unborn child who has reached a probable state of development of 20 weeks after fertilization." The requirements would not have applied during a medical emergency when delaying the procedure would endanger the pregnant woman. Penalties for knowing violations of the act would have included civil penalties. Under the Senate version of the measure, the suspension or revocation of a medical license would also have been possible.

On April 19, 2007, in apparent response to the Court's decision in *Gonzales*, the Freedom of Choice Act was introduced in the House by Representative Jerrold Nadler and in the Senate by Senator Barbara Boxer (H.R. 1964/S. 1173). The measure would have codified the Court's decision in *Roe* by stating that a government may not deny or interfere with a woman's right to choose to bear a child, to terminate a pregnancy prior to viability, or to terminate a pregnancy after viability where termination is necessary to protect the life or health of the woman. The act would have also authorized an aggrieved individual to obtain appropriate relief, including relief against a government, in a civil action.

FY2007 Appropriations

H.J.Res. 20, the Revised Continuing Appropriations Resolution, 2007, was enacted on February 15, 2007 (P.L. 110-5) and provided funding for various federal agencies for the remainder of FY2007.[13] Conditions attached to the availability of FY2006 funds, including those pertaining to abortion, were made applicable to funds appropriated for FY2007 under H.J.Res. 20.

The FY2006 appropriations measures retained longstanding restrictions on the use of federal funds for abortion and abortion-related services. H.R. 3057, the FY2006 Foreign Operations appropriations measure (P.L. 109-102), provided that none of the appropriated funds could be made available to an organization or program that supported or participated in the management of a program of coercive abortion or involuntary sterilization. In addition, appropriated funds were not available for the performance of abortions as a method of family planning, or to motivate or coerce any person to practice abortions. Appropriated funds were not available to lobby for or against abortion. To reduce reliance on abortion in developing nations, funds were available only for voluntary family planning projects which offered a broad range of family planning methods and services. Such voluntary family planning projects were required to meet specified requirements.

Contributions to the United Nations Population Fund (UNFPA) were conditioned on the entity not funding abortions. In addition, amounts appropriated to the UNFPA under the measure were required to be kept in an account that was separate from the UNFPA's other accounts. The UNFPA could not commingle funds provided under the measure with the entity's other sums.

H.R. 2862, the FY2006 appropriations measure for the Departments of Commerce, Justice, and State (P.L. 109-108), prohibited the use of funds to pay for abortions in the federal prison system except in cases where the life of the mother would have been endangered if the fetus was carried to term or in the case of rape.

Under H.R. 3058, the FY2006 appropriations measure for the Departments of Transportation, Treasury, and Housing and Urban Development, the Judiciary, the District of Columbia, and Independent Agencies (P.L. 109-115), appropriated funds could not be used to pay for abortions or for any administrative expenses related to a health plan in the federal employees health benefits program that provided benefits or coverage for abortions. H.R. 3058 also prohibited the use of appropriated and local funds to pay for abortions in the District of Columbia except where the life of the mother would have been endangered if the fetus was carried to term or where the pregnancy was the result of an act of rape or incest.

H.R. 3010, the FY2006 appropriations measure for the Departments of Labor, Health and Human Services, and Education, and Related Agencies (P.L. 109-149), prohibited the use of funds, including funds derived from any trust fund that received appropriations, for abortions except in cases of rape or incest, or where a woman who suffered from a physical disorder, injury, or illness would have her life jeopardized if an abortion was not performed. H.R. 3010 included the nondiscrimination language that first appeared in the FY2005 appropriations provisions for the Department of Health and Human Services. This language prohibited the availability of appropriated funds to a federal agency or program or to a state or local government if such agency, program, or government subjected a health care entity to discrimination on the basis that the entity did not provide, pay for, provide coverage of, or refer for abortions

FY2008 Appropriations

On December 26, 2007, the President signed H.R. 2764, the Consolidated Appropriations Act, 2008 (P.L. 110-161). The measure provided FY2008 funds for all of the federal agencies except the Department of Defense. The Department of Defense Appropriations Act, 2008, was enacted separately on November 13, 2007 (P.L. 110-116).

Longstanding restrictions on the use of federal funds for abortion and abortion-related services were again included in the FY2008 omnibus appropriations measure. For example, H.R. 2764 continued restrictions on the use of funds to pay for abortions in the federal prison system except in cases where the life of the mother would be endangered if the fetus was carried to term or in the case of rape. Subject to similar exceptions, H.R. 2764 continued other restrictions on the use of appropriated funds to pay for the abortions of federal employees or for any administrative expenses related to a health plan in the federal employees health benefits program that provided benefits or coverage for abortions. H.R. 2764 also maintained nondiscrimination language that prohibited the availability of appropriated funds to a federal agency or program or to a state or local government if such agency, program, or government subjected any institutional or individual health care entity to discrimination on the basis that the entity did not provide, pay for, provide coverage of, or refer for abortions.

Although H.R. 2764 was passed by the Senate with a provision that seemed to weaken the socalled "Mexico-City policy," such provision was removed from the final version of the measure. The policy, first announced by President Reagan at the 1984 United Nations International Conference on Population in Mexico City, requires foreign nongovernmental organizations to agree as a condition of receiving federal funds to avoid performing or promoting abortion as a method of family planning. The inclusion of the provision in the Senate-passed version of the bill aroused controversy because it would have permitted foreign nongovernmental organizations to receive federal funds and still perform or promote abortion with their own funds.

End Notes

[1] For additional information on the federal health care conscience protection laws, see CRS Report RL34703, *The History and Effect of Abortion Conscience Clause Laws*, by Jon O. Shimabukuro.

[2] Ensuring That Department of Health and Human Services Funds Do Not Support Coercive or Discriminatory Policies or Practices in Violation of Federal Law, 73 Fed. Reg. 78,072, 78,074 (Dec. 19, 2008) (to be codified at 45 C.F.R. pt. 88).

[3] *Id.*

[4] For additional information on the Congressional Review Act, seeCRS Report RL34747, *Midnight Rulemaking: Considerations for Congress and a New Administration*, by Curtis W. Copeland.

[5] *See id.*

[6] For a more detailed discussion of the relevant case law, seeCRS Report 95-724, *Abortion Law Development: A Brief Overview*, by Jon O. Shimabukuro.

[7] *See Planned Parenthood of Northern New England v. Ayotte*, 571 F.Supp.2d 265 (D. N.H. 2008).

[8] *See also* CRS Report RL30415, *Partial-Birth Abortion: Recent Developments in the Law*, by Jon O. Shimabukuro.

[9] 149 *Cong. Rec.* S2523 (daily ed. February 14, 2003) (statement of Sen. Santorum).

[10] *Id.*

[11] Unlike "as-applied" challenges, which consider the validity of a statute as applied to a particular plaintiff, facial challenges seek to invalidate a statute in all of its applications.

[12] For a review of the full debate on S.J.Res. 3, see 129 Cong. Rec. S9076 *et seq.* (daily ed. June 27, 1983); 129 Cong. Rec. S9265 *et seq.* (daily ed. June 28, 1983).

[13] For additional information on H.J.Res. 20, 110th Cong. (2007), see CRS Report RL33282, *The Budget for Fiscal Year 2007*, by Philip D. Winters.

In: Abortion: Legislative and Legal Issues   ISBN: 978-1-60741-522-0
Editor: Kevin G. Nolan   © 2010 Nova Science Publishers, Inc.

Chapter 3

ABORTION SERVICES AND MILITARY MEDICAL FACILITIES[*]

David F. Burrelli

SUMMARY

In 1993, President Clinton modified the military policy on providing abortions at military medical facilities. Under the change directed by the President, military medical facilities were allowed to perform abortions if paid for entirely with non-Department of Defense (DOD) funds (i.e., privately funded). Although arguably consistent with statutory language barring the use of Defense Department funds, the President's policy overturned a former interpretation of existing law barring the availability of these services. On December 1, 1995, H.R. 2126, the FY1996 DOD appropriations act, became law (P.L. 104-61). Included in this law was language barring the use of funds to administer any policy that permits the performance of abortions at any DOD facility except where the life of the mother would be endangered if the fetus were carried to term or where the pregnancy resulted from an act of rape or incest. Language was also included in the FY1996 DOD Authorization Act (P.L. 104-106, February 10, 1996) prohibiting the use of DOD facilities in the

---

[*] This is an edited, reformatted and augmented version of a CRS Report for Congress publication, Report 95-387F, dated July 10, 2008.

performance of abortions. These served to reverse the President's 1993 policy change. Recent attempts to change or modify these laws have failed.

Over the last three decades, the availability of abortion services at military medical facilities has been subjected to numerous changes and interpretations. Within the last 15 years, Congress has considered numerous amendments to effectuate such changes. Although Congress, in 1992, passed one such amendment to make abortions available at overseas installation, it was vetoed.

The changes ordered by the President did not necessarily have the effect of greatly increasing access to abortion services. Abortions are generally not performed at military medical facilities in the continental United States. In addition, few have been performed at these facilities abroad for a number of reasons. First, the U.S. military follows the prevailing laws and rules of foreign countries regarding abortion. Second, the military has had a difficult time finding health care professionals in uniform willing to perform the procedure.

With the enactment of P.L. 104-61 and P.L. 104-106, these questions became moot, because now, neither DOD funds nor facilities may be used to administer any policy that provides for abortions at any DOD facility, except where the life of the mother may be endangered if the fetus were carried to term. Privately-funded abortions at military facilities are permitted when the pregnancy was the result of an act of rape or incest.

There has been little legislative activity affecting the military on this issue. The last major effort occurred with an amendment to the House version of the FY2007 National Defense Authorization Act would allow DOD facilities outside the U.S. to perform privately-funded abortions. This language was rejected by the conference committee.

PURPOSE

The purpose of this chapter is to describe and discuss the provisions for providing abortion services to military personnel, their dependents and other military health care beneficiaries at military medical facilities. The report describes the history of these provisions, with particular emphasis on legislative actions. Finally, this chapter discusses a number of proposals to modify the law as well as other related legislative and administrative actions.

ISSUE

Shortly after his inauguration on January 20, 1993, President Clinton issued a memorandum on abortions at military hospitals. This memorandum directed a change in policy so that abortions could be performed at military medical facilities provided that the procedure was privately funded. This memo stated that:

> Section 1093 of title 10 of the United States Code prohibits the use of Department of Defense ("DOD") funds to perform abortions except where the life of a women would be endangered if the fetus were carried to term. By memorandum of December 21, 1987, and June 21, 1988, DOD has gone beyond what I am informed are the requirements of the statute and has banned all abortions at U.S. military facilities, even where the procedure is privately funded. The ban is unwarranted. Accordingly, I hereby direct that you reverse the ban immediately and permit abortion services to be provided, if paid for entirely with non-DOD funds and in accordance with other relevant DOD policies and procedures.[1]

The issue at hand was how the language in Title 10 of the United States Code and the President's memo were to be interpreted. As the President's memorandum made obvious, this language has been subject to varying interpretations that allowed or denied abortion services. Specifically, section 1093 states:

> Funds available to the Department of Defense may not be used to perform abortions except where the life of the mother would be endangered if the fetus were carried to term.[2]

Although the President's interpretation of the language was arguably consistent with the letter of the law, critics contend that it countermanded the spirit of the statute and is overly broad. In other words, it is argued that the intent of this language was to prevent the DOD from providing abortion services. Proponents of the Clinton change argued that Congress allowed for exactly this type of interpretation. Proponents note that this interpretation was particularly important for eligible beneficiaries who are deployed overseas in areas where affordable and sanitary abortion services may not be available in the local economy.

Following the election of the 104th Congress, Democrats were replaced by Republicans as committee leaders. Representative Robert K. Dornan, the then-new Republican Chairman of the Military Personnel and Compensation Subcommittee (House National Security Committee), noted that one of his priorities "[was] barring abortions at overseas military hospitals, even if the patients pay for them."[3] On December 1, 1995, P.L. 104-61 was enacted. According to this law:

> Sec. 8119. None of the funds made available in this Act may be used to administer any policy that permits the performance of abortions at medical treatment or other facilities of the Department of Defense.

> Sec. 8119A. The provision of Section 8119 shall not apply where the life of the mother would be endangered if the fetus were carried to term, or the pregnancy is the result of an act of rape or incest.

On February 10, 1996, P.L. 104-106 was enacted. This law further limited that availability of abortion services:

> Sec. 738(b). RESTRICTION ON THE USE OF FACILITIES — No medical treatment facility or other facility of the Department of Defense may be used to perform an abortion except where the life of the mother would be endangered if the fetus were carried to term or in a case in which the pregnancy is the result of an act of rape or incest.[4]

Since then, efforts to modify the law pertaining to abortions have become a routine part of the legislative process.

BACKGROUND

There appears to be no evidence of a formal service policy on abortions prior to 1970. Sources familiar with the issue at that time note that the availability of abortion services at military medical facilities varied by service, location, physician, and "command milieu." Each of the services approached the issue differently. The Air Force tended to be somewhat more liberal, while the Army and the Navy tended to be somewhat more conservative. Each facility also tended to follow the laws and regulations of the state within which it was located. Individual physicians ultimately had a say regarding whether or not they personally would provide such services. Finally, the commanders of various medical facilities may have had some effect on how and under what circumstances abortion services may have been provided. Commanders often lead by example without explicitly stating their own opinions, policies, or giving direct orders. Subordinates are acutely aware of their commander's approach to issues and often will integrate this approach into their own practice. In other words, a policy may exist without one ever being officially stated. Although formal policy may not exist, physicians also follow professional guidelines, as they interpret them, by practicing "good medicine." Thus, the decision to provide an abortion may have been based on a host of medical indications particular to any given case. Generally, it appears that military physicians performed relatively few abortions at military medical facilities in this era.

In certain situations, such as in Vietnam (1961-1975), military medical facilities generally did not provide abortion services. Instead, medical evacuations to other countries that had available procedures (Japan, for example) provided access to abortion services.

In 1970, the office responsible for health affairs at DOD reportedly issued "orders that military hospitals perform abortions when it is medically necessary or when the mental health of the mother is threatened."[5] The rules, however, did not require military personnel to perform abortions. These rules were less restrictive than the abortion laws in a number of states. One year later, then-President Richard M. Nixon directed that military policy concerning abortions at military bases in the United States "be made to correspond with the laws of the States where the bases are located."[6]

Following the 1973 Supreme Court case of *Roe v. Wade*,[7] the Department of Defense funded abortions for any women eligible for DOD health care, subject to certain limitations: first, two physicians were required to find that the abortion was "medically indicated" or required for "reasons of mental health"; second, the funding for these services could not be in conflict with the law of the state in which the abortion is carried out.[8] Since states had differing rules regarding abortion, it was possible for women to be treated differently depending on the location of the facility. Nevertheless, there remains anecdotal evidence of variations in accessibility similar to those that existed before *Roe v. Wade*.

In 1975, concerns were raised over inconsistencies between state statutes and the Roe decision. Military medical personnel were instructed to follow the Constitutional guidance provided in Roe in certain instances, even though the state statutes had not been successfully challenged in court.[9]

From August 31, 1976, to August 31, 1977, approximately 26,000 abortions were performed in military hospitals or in the CHAMPUS program.[10]

In 1978, an amendment to the Department of Defense appropriations bill offered by Representative Robert Dornan prohibited the use of Defense Department funds for abortions with certain exceptions. This amendment, as enacted, stated that:

> None of the funds appropriated by this Act shall be used to perform abortions except where the life of the mother would be endangered if the fetus were carried to term; or except for such medical procedures necessary for the victims of rape or incest, when such rape or incest has been reported promptly to a law enforcement agency or public health service; or except in those instances where severe and long-lasting physical health damage to the mother would result if the pregnancy were carried to term when so determined by two physicians. Nor are payments prohibited for drugs or devices to prevent implantation of the fertilized ovum, or for medical procedures necessary for the termination of an ectopic pregnancy.[11]

In 1979, similar language was enacted in the FY1980 DOD appropriations act. The 1979 language did not contain any restrictions with regard to the "severe and long-lasting physical health damage to the mother that would result if the pregnancy were carried to term when so determined by two physicians." In other words, a determination that carrying the pregnancy to term would affect the physical health of a woman was not a basis for providing abortions under this language.[12]

This language did not prevent all abortions at military hospitals. Military hospitals overseas reportedly performed approximately 1,300 abortions in FY1979. These abortions were privately paid for. Defense officials allowed these procedures under the rationale that at certain overseas (or isolated U.S.) stations, safe and reliable civilian facilities were not always available.[13]

In 1980, the language included in the FY1981 DOD appropriations act was again modified as follows:

> None of the funds appropriated by this Act shall be used to perform abortions except where the life of the mother would be endangered if the fetus were carried to term; or except for such medical procedures necessary for the victim of rape or incest, when such rape has within seventy-two hours been reported to a law enforcement agency or public health service; nor are payments prohibited for drugs or devices to prevent implantation of the fertilized ovum, or for medical procedures necessary for the termination of an ectopic pregnancy: *Provided, however,* That the several States are and shall remain free not to fund abortions to the extent that they in their sole discretion deem appropriate.[14]

Under this language, the reporting requirement for incest was removed. Also, victims of rape were required to report the incident within 72 hours.[15] In addition, language was added encouraging the states to exercise their authority with regard to funding abortions.

The language was shortened considerably in 1981. Many of the exceptions to the prohibition of funding were removed. This language stated that:

> None of the funds provided by this Act shall be used to perform abortions except where the life of the mother would be endangered if the fetus were carried to term.[16]

Identical language was included in the following two years' appropriations acts.[17] Finally, in 1984, Congress codified this language in Title 10, United States Code (see quoted text at the top of page 2).[18]

In 1988, DOD modified its rules to require a physician's statement for abortion claims made via CHAMPUS. This change was instituted to assure that all claims for abortions performed in the private sector and covered by CHAMPUS were for lifethreatening situations. "CHAMPUS officials said life-threatening conditions include leukemia, breast cancer and other malignancies, kidney failure, congestive heart failure, severe heart disease, uncontrolled diabetes and several other conditions."[19]

On June 21, 1988, Dr. William Mayer, then-Assistant Secretary of Defense (Health Affairs), issued a memorandum barring abortions in military medical facilities overseas. Although Dr. Mayer recognized that privately paid abortions did not violate the letter of the law, he issued the memorandum to avoid the appearance of "insensitivity to the spirit" of the law.[20]

In 1990, an attempt to overturn this restriction failed. An amendment (to the DOD authorization act) to allow abortions at military medical facilities overseas was withdrawn when the Senate fell two votes short of the number needed to invoke cloture (58-41).[21] The House of Representatives rejected a similar amendment.

On May 22, 1991, the House of Representatives reversed itself and passed (220-208) an amendment to the DOD authorization act that would have reinstated the prepaid overseas policy. Proponents argued that the language would be merely a return to the policy as it existed prior to Dr. Mayer's memo of 1988. Opponents countered that, as drafted, the amendment offered by Representative AuCoin would go beyond the then-prevailing policy by allowing abortions for any reason and at any time during the pregnancy.[22] The measure was rejected once again when the Senate fell two votes short of the 60 votes needed to invoke cloture (58-40).[23]

The battle over this language intensified. Proponents stated that military women or dependents overseas were forced into dangerous or life-threatening situations in countries where safe, legal, or affordable abortions could not be provided. Opponents argued that no woman was denied military transportation to receive access to an abortion in another country.

Again in 1992, Representative AuCoin introduced language to overturn the restrictions on abortions at overseas military facilities. This amendment was passed (216-193).[24] On September 18, 1992, the Senate rejected (36-55) an effort to strike language overturning the restrictions on overseas abortions. Despite these votes, it was expected that President George H. W. Bush would veto any defense legislation reinstating the former policy. This expected veto was cited as the reason for the language being dropped by the conferees.[25] By unanimous consent, the Senate agreed to substitute the language pertaining to overseas abortions into S. 3144 after striking all after the enacting clause.[26] S. 3144 was simultaneously passed by unanimous consent. The House subsequently passed the measure (220-186) on October 3, 1992.[27]

Arguably, the Senate and House agreed to remove this language from the DOD authorization act in anticipation of a presidential veto. By removing the language and passing it as a free-standing bill, the authorization act was not jeopardized. Since this was not presented in the authorization act, it remains unknown whether President Bush would have exercised his veto authority over the entire bill. Nevertheless, President Bush did pocket-veto S. 3144 on October 31, 1992 (after the congressional adjournment). No attempt was made to override this veto.[28]

As a result of President Clinton's 1993 memorandum (see page 1), then-Secretary of Defense Les Aspin directed the Secretaries of the Military Departments to reinstate the pre-1988 policy concerning the availability of abortions overseas. On May 9, 1994, the Assistant Secretary of Defense (Health Affairs), Dr. Stephen C. Joseph, released a memorandum[29] seeking to unify and make consistent DOD policy. This policy had five parts that 1) provided access to abortion services for service women and eligible dependents overseas, 2) required the valid consent of a parent or other designated person in the case of a minor who was "not mature enough and well enough informed to give valid consent," 3) relieved those medical practitioners directly involved from performing abortions if they objected, 4) respected host nation laws regarding abortion, and, 5) directed the Military Health Services System to provide other means of access if providing pre-paid abortion services at a facility was not feasible. Such alternate means could include supplementing staff with contract personnel, referrals, travel, etc. The cost of an abortion had been reported to be about $500.[30]

In practice, the policy instituted by President Clinton's 1993 action may not have had the effects the President had expected. Although abortion access had been liberalized in terms of overall policy, liberalization had not necessarily occurred in terms of actual access.

> In the six years preceding the 1988 ban, military hospitals overseas had performed an average of 30 abortions annually. Last spring, though, when the military medical officials surveyed 44 Army, Navy and Air Force obstetricians and gynecologists stationed in Europe, they found that all but one doctor adamantly refused to perform the procedure.
>
> That one holdout, too, quickly switched positions.... No military medical personnel willing to perform abortions have stepped forward in the Pentagon's sprawling Pacific theater of operations, either.[31]

A number of reasons have been advanced to explain this general unwillingness by health care personnel in uniform to perform these procedures. First, fewer medical schools require or provide training in these techniques than was the case in the years immediately following the Roe v. Wade decision.[32] Second, it is widely thought that, the military in general, and military physicians in particular, tend to be more conservative on social issues than many population cohorts. Even if training were made available it is unlikely that many would volunteer. Third, the social order on military posts tends to be very close-knit and hierarchical. A subordinate may choose not to "ruffle the feathers" of a superior over such a contentious issue. Thus, the social norms established by superiors in the military environment are likely to translate into action or inaction by subordinates. This conventional wisdom gains credibility given the enormous amount of leverage superiors in the military have over the careers of subordinates. (Although this is true in the civilian context, it apparently exists to a lesser degree, especially in professional fields such as medicine in which civilians are generally unwilling to formally judge or second-guess professional colleagues.) Fourth, the medical team must consist of volunteers. Any member of a medical team needed to perform an abortion can essentially "veto" it. Fifth, since military physicians are paid a salary, and not on the basis of procedures performed, there is no economic incentive to provide abortions. Finally, rules exist requiring the services to respect the prevailing laws in each country. Thus, the restrictions of a particular country may limit the access to pre-paid abortions at military facilities (see Appendix).[33]

Given these factors and considerations, it was reported that 27 abortions were performed at military hospitals worldwide in 1993[34] and 10 in 1994. All of the 1994 abortions were reported to be "life of the mother" cases; i.e., none were "pre-paid." According to data provided by DOD, two abortions were performed at military treatment facilities worldwide in FY1999. For fiscal years 2000, 2001, 2002, 2003, and 2004, the respective number of therapeutic abortions reported was 1, 5, 3, 4, and 3. For fiscal years 2005, 2006 and 2007, the numbers of therapeutic abortion reported were 4, 5 and 5, respectively. Over these 8 years, DOD has performed an average of 3.75 therapeutic abortions per year.

Responding to the lack of medical personnel willing to perform abortions, the Army's 7th Medical Command (Europe) sought in 1993 to hire a civilian physician whose duties would include providing abortion services.[35] This move would have been consistent with the President's memo stating that "[i]n circumstances in which it is not feasible to provide pre-paid abortion services in a particular military facility, the [Military Health Services System] shall develop other means to assure access." Such an affirmative step would have provided access where none was available before. However, such a step could have been viewed as encouraging abortion and threatened to provoke protests both within the uniformed services and in the international community.[36] To date, reports of protests have not been found.

Another consideration along similar lines is to expand the use of foreign physicians, as suggested by the Defense Advisory Committee for Women in the Services (DACOWITS). This may be effective in certain situations, but not all, since DOD is still required to observe local laws. Countries such as Spain, South Korea, and Panama outlaw or sharply restrict abortions.[37]

Following German unification, in 1993, a German court issued an injunction against a law that would have unified abortion policies in the east and west. The *Bundestag*, lower house of the German parliament, struggled to write new laws. During this void, the performance of abortions or restrictions on abortion services at military facilities in Germany, although not illegal, may have been inflammatory to certain German sensitivities.[38] On August 21, 1995, German President Roman Herzog signed into law a measure passed by the *Bundestag* (on June 29) and approved by the *Bundesrat*, upper house, (on July 14). Under this law, abortions are illegal (except in cases of rape or "medical necessity"), but a woman who seeks an abortion during the first 12 weeks of pregnancy will not be subject to criminal prosecution provided she attends a compulsory counseling session reviewing her options.[39]

Contracting with foreign physicians poses its own problems. Countries that lack professional medical personnel trained to U.S. standards (the very reason argued for providing these services in the first place) are less likely to have physicians with a skill level that would be commendable for contracting.

In certain cases, contracting may be an option, but it raises other considerations. If the patient was to pay the cost of the abortion, does such a cost include a pro-rated amount based on contracting, training, travel, and other costs required to provide these services? Inclusion of these in such a cost calculation could well make the price of these services prohibitive. Conversely, using Defense Department funds to make available "pre-paid" abortions (i.e., through contracting, travel, etc.) could be viewed as in conflict with 10 U.S.C. 1093.

According to a DOD Information Paper, in August 1994, "a policy on hiring non-military physicians to perform abortions was issued with specific reference to treatment facilities in Germany. DoD respects host nation laws regarding abortion."[40]

Furthermore, it was unlikely that abortion services would become more available if the military reduced the number of physicians as part of DOD downsizing of the force structure. One drawdown proposal suggests that DOD could reduce the number of physicians in uniform by as much as 50%.[41] Under the Administration's long-term defense spending plans, 5,600 civilian medical personnel will be cut from the Army over the next six years. The Navy and Air Force, together, are expected to be reduced by less than 2,000. These reductions "amount to the equivalent of shutting three of the Army's eight medical centers, experts say."[42] The reduction of civilian professionals in the U.S. military may require DOD to rotate uniformed physicians back to the U.S. from overseas, further reducing the number of physicians overseas. Such a reduction would likely serve to reduce the availability of abortion services overseas.

On May 29, 2002, a federal judge ruled that the military must pay for a 1994 abortion of an anencephalic fetus.[43] Later, in August 2002, a second federal court ruled likewise in a separate case involving another anencephalic fetus.[44] Both cases were reversed on appeal.[45]

"PLAN B" AND RU-486

In February 2002, the DOD Pharmacy and Therapeutics (P&T) Executive Council recommended adding levonorgestrel, aka "Plan B," to the Basic Core Formulary,[46] subject to further review. Plan B is described as an emergency contraceptive used to prevent pregnancy following a known or suspected contraceptive failure (e.g. broken condom) or when a pregnancy may result because no contraception was used (e.g. rape). It is noted that it will not terminate an "established pregnancy." In other words, it is not RU-486, a known abortifacient, which chemically induces an abortion. RU-486 is subject to restrictions under 10 U.S.C. § 1093.[47]

According to a DOD Information Paper, Plan B could possibly "prevent a pregnancy by interfering with ovulation, sperm transport through cervical mucus and fallopian tubes, release of pituitary gonadotropins, corpus luteum functions, fertilization, *embryo transport and implantation*."[48] [emphasis added] The possibility of preventing a fertilized egg from implanting leads to the argument, for those who maintain that life begins at conception, that Plan B represents a potential form of abortion in certain cases. In May 2002, the P&T Executive Council Meeting released the following:

> At the February 2002 DOD Pharmacy & Therapeutics (P&T) Executive Council meeting, the Council recommended the addition of levonorgestrel 0.75 mg (Plan B) to the Basic Core Formulary (BCF), subject to the review of the Director, TRICARE Management Activity (TMA) and/or the Assistance Secretary of Defense for Health Affairs (ASD(HA)). On 28 March 2002, the Executive Director of TMA signed an Action Memo approving the recommendation. On April 3, 2002 the co-chair of the DOD P&T Committee informed the Council members and pharmacy consultants of the decision, and re-informed the Council on 7 May 2002. On 8 May 2002 the Executive Council was reconvened briefly to announce that the Council co-chairs had been informed that the ASD(HA) also wanted to review the Council's recommendation and that the Executive Director of TMA had rescinded his earlier approval. Therefore, Plan B has NOT been approved for addition to the BCF at this time, and the ASD(HA) is reviewing the Council's recommendation. [Military Treatment Facilities] MTFs are required to include all BCF drugs on their local formularies. As a result of Plan B's removal from the BCF, each MTF's P&T committee must now re-evaluate whether this product is within the scope of practice at the MTF and whether the MTF wants to continue to have Plan B on its formulary.[49]

In May 2005, a proposed amendment to make Plan B available on all military bases died in the House Rules Committee (as part of its consideration of the FY2005 National Defense Authorization Act).[50] This is not to say that Plan B is not available at certain military bases or to military health care beneficiaries. On September 7, 2005, it was reported that certain military bases do have Plan B on hand and have offered it, usually in cases of sexual assault, but also in cases where other contraceptives failed or unprotected sex was involved. Further, military physicians may prescribe the medication allowing the beneficiary to have the prescription filled at civilian pharmacies.[51]

Although tangentially relevant to DOD policy, Plan B has been the subject of controversy within the Food and Drug Administration (FDA):

> FDA Commissioner Lester Crawford on August 26 [2005] said the agency is indefinitely deferring Barr Laboratories' application for nonprescription sales of its emergency contraceptive Plan B and opening a 60-day public comment period on the application sparking charges that the decision was motivated by politics rather than science, ... FDA in May 2004 issued a "not approvable" letter in response to Barr's original application to allow Plan B – which can prevent pregnancy if taken within 72 hours of sexual intercourse – to be sold without a doctor's prescription and in January delayed a ruling on Barr's revised application, which would allow EC to be sold without a doctor's prescription only to women ages 17 and older. During a confirmation hearing in March, Crawford told the Senate committee that FDA would approve the application "within weeks."[52]

On August 24, 2006, the FDA approved over-the-counter sales of Plan B to women 18 years old and older.[53] Nearly three months later, Plan B began appearing in drug stores.[54]

Although this latter controversy is not directly related to the Department of Defense, it appears that the decision made by the FDA was taken into consideration by DOD officials with regard to emergency contraceptives.

According to the DOD Pharmacoeconomic Center, Plan B is not on the Basic Core Formulary, but Military Treatment Facilities may have it as part of their formulary.[55]

"PARENTAL NOTIFICATION"

"Parental notification" is concerned with those instances in which an abortion is sought at a military facility by or on behalf of a military dependent who is a minor and/or incapable of making such a decision.

According to DOD:

> Assuming that an abortion is authorized [under statute], consent must be obtained before any surgical procedure is performed. The requirement to obtain consent is required in military treatment facilities (MTFs), because the standard of care for medical practice in MTFs within the United States is governed by the Federal Tort Claims Act (FTCA). The standard of care for obtaining consent under FTCA is that the provider will follow state law governing the circumstances under which a minor may consent for medical treatment. In overseas facilities, consent by minors for abortions is governed by [DOD] Health Affairs Policy dated May 9, 1994, as amended by [DOD] Health Affairs Policy 96-030, dated February 13, 1996. Those policies state that the host nation laws or legal requirements will apply. In the absence of such host nation laws or legal requirements, valid consent for minors may be obtained in either of two methods. First, the consent of at least one parent or guardian is provided. Second, the commanding officer of the medical treatment facility (or if the commanding officer is not a physician, a senior physician designated by the commanding officer) makes a judgment, upon the recommendation of the attending physician, that the minor is mature enough and well enough informed to give valid consent, or, if she is not sufficiently mature and informed, that the desired abortion would be in her best interest.[56]

LEGISLATIVE ACTION SINCE 1995

The House version of the FY1996 Defense Authorization Act contained a section that would terminate the policy of allowing the performance of abortions on a pre-paid basis, at military facilities. Under this language:

> This section would amend Section 1093 of Title 10, United States Code, to include restricting the Department of Defense from using medical treatment facilities or other DOD facilities, as well as DOD funds, to perform abortions unless necessary to save the life of the mother.[57]

The Senate report contained no similar provisions.

As a result of numerous political differences between the House and the Senate language, as well as Administration opposition on a number of issues raising the specter of a veto, the authorization act stalled in conference. Legislators sought to have language included in the FY1996 DOD appropriations act that would prohibit abortions at overseas military facilities. The Appropriations Conference Committee originally included the following language:

> Sec. 8119. None of the funds made available in this Act may be used to administer any policy that permits the performance of abortions at medical treatment or other facilities of the Department of Defense, except when it is made known to the federal official having authority to obligate or expend such funds that the life of the mother would be endangered if the fetus were carried to term: Provided, That the provisions of this section shall enter into force if specifically authorized in the National Defense Authorization Act for Fiscal Year 1996.

Thus, the nature of this language only allowed it to take effect, when and if the authorization language was enacted into law. As noted, at the time, the authorization bill was stalled in conference and faced a possible veto. The failure of the authorization bill to be passed would negate any language concerning abortions in the appropriations bill.

On September 29, 1995, pro-life legislators in the House and a large number of Democrats (opposed to the bill on policy and other spending considerations) joined ranks and rejected the conference version of the FY1996 DOD appropriations act (151-267), thereby returning the bill to the House-Senate conference.[58] On November 16, 1995, the conferees agreed to a compromise that included the following language:

> Sec. 8119. None of the funds made available in this Act may be used to administer any policy that permits the performance of abortions at medical treatment or other facilities of the Department of Defense.
> Sec. 8119A. The provision of Section 8119 shall not apply where the life of the mother would be endangered if the fetus were carried to term, or the pregnancy is the result of an act of rape or incest.

On December 1, 1995, the appropriations act, with the above two sections, became law.[59]

On December 15, 1995, the House passed the FY1996 Authorization Act (containing the language cited on page 13). The bill was approved by the

Senate on December 19, 1995. On December 28, 1995, the President vetoed the authorization act, and in a letter to Congress, he stated:

> H.R. 1530 [FY1996 Defense Authorization Act] also contains ... provisions that would unfairly affect certain service members.... I remain very concerned about provisions that would restrict service women and female dependents of military personnel from obtaining privately funded abortions in military facilities overseas, except in the cases of rape, incest, or danger to the life of the mother. In many countries, these U.S. facilities provide the only accessible, safe source for these medical services. Accordingly, I urge Congress to repeal a similar provision that became law in the "Department of Defense appropriations act, 1996."[60]

On January 3, 1996, the House of Representatives failed to override the veto with a vote of 240-156. Two days later, the House amended S. 1124 by striking "all after the enacting clause of S. 1124 and insert[ing] in lieu thereof the text of H.R. 1530 [the vetoed language] as reported by the committee of conference on December 13, 1995, contained in [H.Rept. 104-406]."[61] Under unanimous consent, the language was taken from the Speaker's table, as amended, and sent to conference. On January 22, conference report H.Rept. 104-450 was filed. On January 24, 1996, the House agreed to the conference report (287-129). Two day later, the Senate agreed to the conference report (56-34). Provisions barring the use of DOD facilities to perform abortions, except in cases of rape, incest or where the life of the mother would be endangered if the fetus were carried to term or in a case in which the pregnancy, were included in this language (see quoted text at the bottom of page 2). On February 10, 1996, President Clinton signed the FY1996 Defense Authorization Act into law.[62]

Although the prohibition against using funding in the appropriations act would have lapsed at the end of the fiscal year, the change made via the authorization act modifies Title 10 United States Code. As such, this change will not lapse at the end of the fiscal year. Thus, this language will stay in effect unless and until Congress (with the President's signature) specifically acts to amend, modify, strengthen or repeal these provisions.

On May 14, 1996, an amendment was offered to the House version of the FY1997 National Defense Authorization Act to overturn the prohibition on military facilities performing abortions and allow such abortions to be performed at these medical facilities so long as federal funds are not used (i.e., patient-paid abortions). The amendment was defeat by a vote of 192 ayes and 225 noes.[63] Slightly more than one month later, the Senate passed an identical amendment to its version of the FY1997 National Defense Authorization Act by a voice vote.[64] Ultimately, the Senate conferees receded and the Senate amendment was dropped.

Efforts to amend these provisions have continued. On June 19, 1997, Representative Jane Harman offered an amendment to the FY1998 DOD Authorization Act that would purportedly

> [restore the] policy affording access to certain health care procedures for female members of the armed forces and dependents at Department of Defense facilities.

The amendment was rejected (196-224).[65]

In 1998, the House National Security Committee rejected another attempt to allow for privately funded abortions at these facilities.[66] On June 25, 1998, the Senate rejected a similar provision (44-49).[67]

During consideration of the FY2000 National Defense Authorization Act, the House Personnel Subcommittee accepted an amendment by Representative Loretta Sanchez to reverse the restrictions on privately funded abortions being performed at overseas military medical facilities. Another amendment, by Representative Kuykendall, would have allowed Defense Department funding of abortions in cases of rape or incest. Upon consideration by the House Armed Services Committee, the Sanchez amendment was dropped and the Kuykendall amendment was further amended by Representative Buyer. As amended, the Kuykendall amendment would allow Defense Department funding of abortions in cases of *forcible* rape or incest *provided that the rape or incest had been reported to a law enforcement agency.* [Italics represent the Buyer changes.] Later efforts to reinstate the Sanchez language allowing for abortions at overseas military facilities when personal funds are used were rejected by both the House and the Senate. Ultimately, the Kuykendall amendment, as amended, was also deleted during conference consideration of the FY2000 National Defense Authorization Act, thereby leaving the law unchanged.[68]

Although not specifically related to the above discussion of the military abortion issue, other language has been proposed that would have had an effect on the consideration of the abortion issue. H.R. 2436[69] included, in part, language modifying Title 10, United States Code. According to this language, any conduct violating certain provisions of the Uniform Code of Military

Justice, by a person subject to the Uniform Code of Military Justice, that causes death or bodily injury to a fetus who is in utero at the time the conduct takes place, would be guilty of a criminal offense. For example, if during an assault on a pregnant women, the fetus were injured, such an injury would constitute a separate offense. Exceptions were included in cases of abortions, medical treatment of the woman, or conduct of the woman with regard to her fetus. On September 30, 1999, the House passed this language (254-172). The next day, it was received and read in the Senate. On February 23, 2000, the Senate Committee on Judiciary held hearings on a Senate companion bill, S. 1673. No further action was then taken by the Senate, and the legislation failed to become law. (Similar language was considered in 2004; see "Unborn Victim of Violence Act 2004," below.)

Proponents note that such language would recognize the victimization of the child while in utero and afford appropriate criminal sanctions to perpetrators of violent acts. Critics view the inclusion of such language as a means of defining a fetus as a victim and thereby acknowledging or creating a separate human existence. These critics are concerned that such language would arguably recognize the fetus as separate person in the eyes of the law thereby complicating the abortion debate.[70]

In consideration of the FY2001 National Defense Authorization Act (H.R. 4205), the House Armed Services Committee "voted to retain its ban on abortions at military hospitals unless the mother's life is at risk. The 31-20 vote came May 10, 2000, on an amendment that would have allowed abortions at overseas hospitals if patients rather than the government paid for them. The 29-26 vote came on a failed try to allow military hospitals to perform abortions in cases of rape or incest."[71] Eight days later, a floor amendment was offered that would strike subsections a and b of 10 USC § 1093, effectively removing any restriction to providing abortions under this title. The amendment was defeated (221-195).[72]

On June 20, 2000, the Senate tabled (50-49) an amendment to the FY2001 National Defense Authorization Act, S. 2549, that would strike Section b of 10 USC § 1093. The amendment would have lifted the ban on the use of military facilities in performing abortions. Although proponents noted that the amendment "would lift restrictions on privately funded abortions at military facilities overseas," as written, the amendment would affect such facilities in the United States as well.[73]

On September 25, 2001, Representative Loretta Sanchez offered an amendment to the National Defense Authorization Act for FY2002. This amendment would have limited the restriction on the use of DOD facilities for performing abortions at those facilities "in the United States." In other words, this language would remove the restriction of providing privately funded abortion services at DOD facilities overseas. The amendment was rejected (199-217).[74]

During debate on the Bob Stump FY2003 National Defense Authorization Act, the Senate (52-40) passed an amendment that would remove the restriction on the use of military facilities.[75] The House had earlier rejected a similar measure (215-202).[76] In a letter to Senator Carl Levin, then-Chairman of the Armed Services Committee, Secretary of Defense Donald H. Rumsfeld wrote:

> The Senate bill removes the current statutory prohibition on access to abortion services at Department of Defense (DoD) medical facilities. The President's senior advisors would recommend that the President veto the bill if it changes current law.[77]

The Senate amendment was dropped by the conference committee.[78]

On April 1, 2004, President Bush signed H.R. 1997, "Unborn Victims of Violence Act of 2004 (Laci and Conner's Law)" into law.[79] Although intended to protect fetuses, this legislation contains a provision that would not permit the prosecution "of any person for conduct relating to an abortion" in which consent was legally obtained or implied.

Amendments to the FY2004 National Defense Authorization Act to modify the law were also offered. In the House, an amendment that would have limited the restriction on DOD facilities to the United States was rejected (201-227).[80]

Likewise the Senate rejected (48-51) an amendment that would have repealed the restriction on using DOD facilities, in general.[81]

However, the Senate agreed, subject to certain limitations, to consider legislation, S. 1104,[82] "to provide for parental involvement in abortions of dependent children of the Armed Forces." The legislation was placed on the Legislative Calendar[83] but failed to be called to the floor.

Consideration of the Ronald W. Reagan FY2005 National Defense Authorization Act included a number of amendments regarding abortion services. In the House of Representatives, Representative Susan A. Davis introduced an amendment that would allow military personnel and their dependents to use their own funds to obtain abortion services at overseas military hospitals. This amendment was defeated (202-221).[84]

In the Senate, an amendment offered by Senator Barbara Boxer, would allow DOD funding of abortions in cases of rape or incest. This amendment, along with 25 other amendments, was passed *en bloc* by unanimous consent.[85] On October 8, 2004, the Conference Report for this legislation noted that the "Boxer amendm ent" had been dropped.[86]

Two other Senate amendments to the Ronald W. Reagan FY2005 National Defense Authorization Act (H.R. 4200) were submitted. The first, S.A. 3406 (Senators Frist and Brownback), would "provide for parental involvement in the performance of abortions for dependent children of members of the Armed Forces." The second, S.A. 3407 (Senators Frist and Brownback), would require the notification of authorities regarding the identity of perpetrators, where possible, in cases of rape or incest when abortions are sought at military facilities. Neither S.A. 3406 nor S.A. 3407 was called up.

In conclusion, under current law, 10 U.S.C. § 1093, Performance of Abortions: Restrictions

(a) Restriction on Use of Funds. — Funds available to the Department of Defense may not be used to perform abortions except where the life of the mother would be endangered if the fetus were carried to term.

(b) Restriction on Use of Facilities. — No medical treatment facility or other facility of the Department of Defense may be used to perform an abortion except where the life of the mother would be endangered if the fetus were carried to term or in a case in which the pregnancy is the result of an act of rape or incest.

On May 25, 2005, the House of Representatives considered an amendment (offered by Representative Susan Davis) to the National Defense Authorization Act for Fiscal Year 2006 (H.R. 1815). The amendment would allow overseas military facilities to provide privately funded abortions for women who are in the miliary or are military dependents. This amendment was rejected (194-233).[87]

On July 25, 2005, Senator Lautenberg filed an amendment in the Senate that would 'restore the previous policy regarding restrictions on the use of medical treatment facilities or other Department of Defense facilities.' This amendment would strike section 1093(b) of title 10 U.S.C. (and remove the title language "Restriction on Use of Funds.–" from section 1093(a)). No further action has been taken on this amendment.[88]

Legislative Action

On May 10, 2006, the House of Representatives considered an amendment (offered by Representative Robert E. Andrews) to the John Warner FY2007 National Defense Authorization Act that would allow overseas military facilities to provide privately funded abortions for women who are in the miliary or are military dependents. This amendment was rejected (191-237).

APPENDIX

According to Department of Defense and individual command officials (as reported to the *Army Times*, September 5, 1994: 18; source: Defense Department and individual command officials), the availability of abortion services (prior to the restrictions enacted on December 1, 1995) at military facilities overseas could vary depending on location.

Germany

National policy: See discussion on page 10 above.

Local U.S. military policy: Under German law, abortions are illegal except in cases of rape or medical necessity. Abortions carried out during the first twelve weeks of pregnancy are not considered a prosecutable offense provided the woman has certification attesting to receiving state approved counseling to review her options. The military does not allow abortions at its facilities.

Since the U.S. ban was lifted: Estimates of how many American service women or family members received abortions from German providers in 1993 are as high as 1,500, although German officials say there is no way to confirm this number.

Italy

National policy: Abortions are permitted. They must be performed by a licensed gynecologist.

Local U.S. military policy: Abortion services comparable to those in the United States are available from Italian providers in the Naples and Sigonella areas. Service women and family members who desire abortions are referred to pre-identified licensed local providers. Abortions are not performed at military hospitals.

Since the U.S. ban was lifted: One elective abortion was reportedly provided in Sigonella at an Italian facility.

Japan

National policy: Abortion is legal and fairly unrestricted, but more expensive than in the United States.

Local U.S. military policy: Given that abortions are readily available in the Japanese community, women seeking abortion from Navy hospitals here are referred to family-service counselors for referrals to Japanese doctors.

Since the U.S. ban was lifted: Few, if any, abortions were performed at military hospitals, Navy officials said. The number of abortions by civilian doctors is unknown.

Korea

National policy: Abortion is illegal except to save the life of the mother.

Local U.S. military policy: The U.S. military's rules for Korea could not be learned from military officials, but because of the local law, abortions would not be available at U.S. hospitals.

Since the U.S. ban was lifted: Service members or family members continue to have to travel outside of Korea to obtain an abortion.

Problematic Comparisons to Foreign Military Policies

Abortion policies of foreign militaries vary. These variations depend on the country's general policy regarding abortion. For instance, abortion policies are affected by religion (Vatican, Israel, and Islamic nations, for example), population control policies (China) and other cultural factors (nationalized health care policies, such as are found in Great Britain), and issues pertaining to the structure of the military — the presence of women in uniform (many Islamic countries do not have women in uniform, making the issue moot). Some countries do not have a military (Costa Rica for instance does not have a military per se but rather a paramilitary style security force). In addition, internal legal restrictions or rulings, such as court rulings on abortion (see Germany), affect the country's policy. Finally, very few countries maintain a level of overseas deployments that make direct comparisons relevant. For these reasons, comparisons to foreign nations in terms of their abortion policy in general, and their policy regarding military abortions at overseas military medical facilities are difficult to justify and of questionable utility.

End Notes

[1] President William J. Clinton, Memorandum for the Secretary of Defense, Memorandum on Abortions in Military Hospitals, January 22, 1993; filed with the Office of the Federal Register, 11:50 a.m., January 27, 1993; cited in Public Papers of the Presidents of the United States, William J. Clinton, 1993, Washington, D.C., Government Printing Office, 1994: 11.

[2] 10 U.S.C. Sec. 1093, added P.L. 98-525, Sec. 1401(e)(5), October 19, 1984, 98 Stat. 2617. It should be noted that the Civilian Health and Medical Program of the Uniformed Services (CHAMPUS), a medical program for military dependents, certain retirees and their dependents who are unable to receive care at a military medical facility, will provide coverage for abortions only when the mother's life is in danger. "The attending physician must certify in writing that the abortion was performed because a life-endangering condition existed, and must provide medical documentation to the CHAMPUS claims processor in order for CHAMPUS to share the cost of the procedure." See U.S. Department of Defense, OCHAMPUS, CHAMPUS Handbook, October 1994: 42.

[3] Maze, Rick, "Representative Dornan: 'Pay gap one of top concerns,'" Army Times, January 16, 1995: 3.

[4] U.S. Congress, Conference Committee, National Defense Authorization Act for Fiscal Year 1996, H.Rept. 104-450, S. 1124, 104th Cong., 2nd Sess., January 22, 1996: 206-207.

[5] Wolffe, Jim, "Abortion ban may be lifted soon stateside," Air Force Times, April 12, 1993: 23.

[6] Statement about Policy on Abortions at Military Base Hospitals in the United States, April 3, 1971, Public Papers of the Presidents of the United States, Richard Nixon, 1971, Washington: GPO,1972) p. 500. Since CHAMPUS (the point of service contract health care for non-active duty beneficiaries — now known as TRICARE Standard) relied, then as now, on local health care providers, these individuals were already subject to State laws and regulations pertaining to abortion.

[7] Roe v. Wade, 410 U.S. 113 (1973). The Court held that the Constitution protects a woman's decision whether or not to terminate pregnancy and that a State may not unduly burden the exercise of that fundamental right by regulations that prohibit or substantially limit access to the means of effectuating that decision.

[8] Ayres, B. Drummond, Jr., New York Times, August 10, 1978: 79 (microfilm).

[9] U.S. Department of Defense, Assistant Secretary of Defense (Health and Environment), James R. Cowen, Memorandum for the Assistant Secretaries of the Military Departments (M&RA), Abortion Policy, September 17, 1975.

[10] U.S. Department of Defense, Directorate for Defense Information, Press Division, 9 August, 1978.

[11] P.L. 95-457, Section 863, October 13, 1978, 92 Stat. 1254. In anticipation of this change, the Office of the Assistant Secretary of Defense (Public Affairs) published a News Release (September 29, 1978) functionally implementing this language effective September 30, 1978. This change also affected funding for CHAMPUS claims.

[12] P.L. 96-154, Section 762, December 21, 1979, 93 Stat. 1162.

[13] Smith, Paul, "1300 FY79 O'seas Abortions Revealed," *Army Times*, December 8, 1980: 2.

[14] P.L. 96-527, Section 760, December 15, 1980, 94 Stat. 3091.

[15] Previous language required that such a report should be made "promptly." DOD interpreted this to mean within 48 hours. It was also expected that victims of incest would report the incident(s) to appropriate authorities, however, the lack of a time restriction meant that a report could be delayed indefinitely. (See "DOD Issues New Rules On Abortion," *Army Times*, March 9, 1981: 15.)

[16] P.L. 97-114, Section 757, December 29, 1981, 95 Stat. 1588.

[17] P.L. 97-377, Section 755, December 21, 1982, 96 Stat. 1860; P.L. 98-212, Section 751, December 8, 1983, 97 Stat. 1447.

[18] 10 U.S.C. 1093, P.L. 98-525, sec 1401(e)(5), October 19, 1984, 98 Stat. 2617. Note this change occurred via an authorization act and not as a part of the appropriations process (*Omnibus Defense Authorization Act, 1985*).

[19] Kimble, Vesta, "Doctor's Statement Needed for Abortion Claims," *Navy Times*, March 14, 1988: 24.

[20] "Abortion Is Restricted At Military Hospitals," *New York Times*, July 19, 1988: A11. "The abortion issue in military hospitals has a symbolic and political importance that dwarfs the actual numbers of people involved. Military hospitals overseas performed only six abortions in the last year they were permitted [1987]." Willis, Grant, "Clinton Ends Ban on Military Abortions," *Air Force Times*, February 1, 1993: 4.

[21] Congressional Record, August 3, 1990: S11813-S11824.

[22] Congressional Record, May 22, 1991: H3394 et seq.

[23] Nelson, Soraya, "Overseas Abortion Amendment Fails," *Army Times* December 1991: 16.

[24] Congressional Record, June 4, 1992: H4150-H4156.

[25] Dewar, Helen, "Bush's Veto Power Stalled the Abortion-Rights Push in Congress," *Washington Post*, November 30, 1991: A6.

[26] Both House and Senate versions of the FY1993 Defense Authorization Act contained provisions that would "entitle military personnel and their dependents to reproductive health care services in a medical facility of the uniformed services outside the United States on a reimbursement basis.... The conferees agree to exclude this provision. The Senate has passed a bill (S. 3144) that contains this provision. The House intends to pass this bill and send it to the President as soon as possible." U.S. Congress, House Conference Committee, National Defense Authorization Act for Fiscal Year 1993, H.Rept. 102-966, H.R. 5006, 102d Cong., 2nd Sess., October 1, 1992: 716.

[27] See H.Res. 589, Congressional Record, October 2, 1992: H10803-H10804, and Congressional Record, October 3, 1992: H10966-H10975.

[28] Congressional Quarterly, December 19, 1992: 3926.

[29] U.S. Department of Defense, Assistant Secretary of Defense (Health Affairs), Memorandum, Implementation of Policy Regarding Pre-Paid Abortions in Military Treatment Facilities, May 9, 1994: 2p.

[30] Nelson, Soraya S., "Pentagon Pens Rules on Abortion," *Army Times*, May 23, 1994: 10.

[31] Morrison, David C., "An Order That Didn't Take," *National Journal*, April 16, 1994: 900.

[32] According to the Alan Guttmacher Institute, from 1976 to 1991, the proportion of residency programs that did not offer abortion training rose from 7.5 to 31%. In 1976, 26% of the residency programs required abortion training. By 1991, only 12% required such training. The Accreditation Council for Graduate Medical Education has directed obstetrical residents should be taught how to perform abortions, unless they have a moral or religious objection. This change in policy is scheduled to become effective on January 1, 1996. Abortion mandated for OB training, Washington Times, February 15, 1995: A12. On March 19, 1996, the Senate passed the Coats amendment (no. 3513): "to amend the Public Health Service Act to prohibit governmental discrimination in the training and licensing of health professionals on the basis of the refusal to undergo or provide training in the performance of induced abortions," by a vote of 63 yeas and 37 nays. Congressional Record, March 19, 1996, S2262-S2266, S2268-S2276, S2280.

[33] "Most countries where American military personnel are stationed restrict or outlaw them [abortions] altogether." Nelson, Soraya S., "Limits Remain on Abortions at Overseas Hospitals," Navy Times, February 22, 1993: 11.

[34] Nelson, Soraya S., "Military Abortions Overseas: Still Rare," Army Times, September 5, 1994: 18.

[35] Scholar, Steve, "Army Seeking Civilian Doctor Willing To Do abortions at Military Hospitals," Stars and Stripes (European), April 28, 1993: 1.

[36] "A Pentagon Decision To Send Doctors Overseas To Perform Abortions in Military Hospitals Could Spark Protest from Pro-Life Groups in Germany, Pro-Life GIs say," Pro-Life Protests, American Legion, July 1994: 10.

[37] "Women in the services," Fast Track, Army Times, July 4, 1994: 20.

[38] "Women's groups, opposition politicians from the west, and easterners across the political spectrum expressed outrage at the court's decision. Many observers felt the decision exposed the deep east-west social divide." CRS Issue Brief IB91018, German-American Relations in the New Europe, by Karen E. Donfried , January 27, 1994, p. 6 (out-of-print; available from author at 78033).

[39] The Week in Germany, January 30, 1998.

[40] Memorandum for Assistant Secretary of Defense (Health Affairs), Information Paper on abortion policy for Dr. Hambre's confirmation hearing, July 1997.

[41] "In June [1994], a Pentagon study found that only about half of the current number of military doctors are needed for any foreseeable military operation." Jowers, Karen, "50% Cut Is Planned in Military Doctors," Air Force Times, January 23, 1995: 28.

[42] Nelson, Soraya S., "Medicare Users May Lose Hospital Access," Navy Times, September 5, 1994: 26.

[43] Britell v. United States, 204 F.Supp.2d 182, May 29, 2002.

[44] Ostrom, Carol M., "Judge: Navy Must Cover Women's Abortion," Seattle Times, August 13, 2002. The 9th Circuit Court of Appeals, without comment, denied a last minute appeal in this case. "Court Rejects Effort to Stop Navy Funding of Abortion," Baltimore Sun, August 18, 2002.

[45] Britell v. United States, 372 F.3d 1370, June 24, 2004, and Doe v. USA, et al., civil docket for case #: 2:02-cv-01657-TSZ, August 18, 2005.

[46] The Basic Core Formulary or BCF refers to those pharmaceuticals that DOD makes available at DOD pharmacies.

[47] Legislation was offered in the 109th Congress (S. 511, Senator DeMint, March 3, 2005 and H.R. 1079, Rep. Bartlett) "To provide that the approved application under the Federal Food, Drug, and Cosmetic Act for the drug commonly known as RU-486 is deemed to have been withdrawn, to provide for the review by the Comptroller General of the United States of the process by which the Food and Drug Administration approved such drug, and for other purposes." Both bills were referred to Committees and have received no further action.

[48] Col. Daniel Remund, Co-chair, DOD Pharmacy & Therapeutics Committee, Information Paper, April 11, 2002.

[49] Department of Defense, Pharmaeconomic Center, Minutes of the DOD Pharmacy & Therapeutics Executive Council Meeting, May 7, 2002, pp. 2-3.

[50] The proposal was similar to language contained in H.R. 2635, Rep. Michael H. Michaud, May 25, 2005.

[51] Montgomery, Nancy, Army Hospitals in Europe Offering 'Morning-After' Pill, *Stars and Stripes* (European edition), June 8, 2005.

[52] "FDA: Indefinitely Defers Decision on Emergency Contraceptive; Plan B," *National Journal Group, Inc.*, September 6, 2005

[53] Harris, Gardiner, F.D.A. Approves Broader Access t Next-Day Pill, *New York Times*, August 25, 2006: 1.

[54] Payne, January W., For Plan B, A Broader Reach, *Washington Post*, November 21, 2006: F1.

[55] DOD, MTF Formulary Management For Contraceptives (Updated 26 Jan 07).

[56] Letter from Speight, Cynthia, CIV, OASD(HA)TMA to Richard Best, CRS, May 28, 2003.

[57] U.S. Congress, House Committee on National Security, National Defense Authorization Act for Fiscal Year 1996, H.Rept. 104-131, H.R. 1530, 104th Cong., 1st Sess., June 1, 1995: 37.

[58] Maze, Rick, and William Matthew, "Defense Spending Bill Slapped Back by Unlikely Union in Congress," *Army Times*, October 9, 1995: 25.

[59] P.L. 104-61, 109 Stat. 636, December 1, 1995.

[60] Veto message from the President of the United States (H. Doc. No. 104-155), cited in the Congressional Record, January 3, 1996: H12.

[61] Congressional Record, January 5, 1996: H302.

[62] P.L. 104-106, 110 Stat. 186, February 10, 1996.

[63] Congressional Record, May 14,1996, H5013-H5022.

[64] Congressional Record, June 19, 1996, S6460-S6469.

[65] Congressional Record, June 19, 1997, H4056-H4069.

[66] CQ Weekly, Other Policy Issues, May 9, 1998: 1240.

[67] Congressional Record, June 25, 1998, S7060-S7076.

[68] Maze, Rick, "Abortion Provision Dropped from Defense Bill," *Times*, August 16, 1999: 11.

[69] H.R. 2436, Representative Linsey Graham, July 1, 1999.

[70] For additional information on the legal aspects of the abortion issue, see CRSReport RL33467, *Abortion: Legislative Response*, by Jon O. Shimabukuro and Karen L. Lewis.

[71] FastTrack, *Times*, May 29, 2000: 6.

[72] Congressional Record, May 18, 2000: H3347-H3350, H3371.

[73] Congressional Record, June 20, 2000: S5406-S5421, S5425.

[74] Congressional Record, September 25, 2001: H6022-25, H6032-33.

[75] Congressional Record, June 21, 2002: S5882.

[76] Congressional Record, May 9, 2002: H2380.

[77] Letter from Secretary of Defense Donald H. Rumsfeld to the Honorable Carl Levin, September 24, 2002.

[78] Congressional Record, November 12, 2002: H8462.

[79] P.L. 108-212; 1185 Stat. 568; April 1, 2004.

[80] Congressional Record, May 22, 2003: H4571.

[81] Congressional Record, May 22, 2003: S6911.

[82] Senator Brownback, May 22, 2003.

[83] Congressional Record, May 22, 2003: D576. See also, "Congress Votes to Keep the Abortion Ban on Bases," Washington Post, May 23, 2003: A7.

[84] Congressional Record, May 19, 2004: H3358.

[85] Congressional Record, June 22, 2004: S7152.

[86] Congressional Record, October 8, 2004: H9549.

[87] Congressional Record, May 25, 2005: H4009-H4013, H4017.

[88] Congressional Record, July 25, 2005, S8845.

In: Abortion: Legislative and Legal Issues   ISBN: 978-1-60741-522-0
Editor: Kevin G. Nolan   © 2010 Nova Science Publishers, Inc.

Chapter 4

EMERGENCY CONTRACEPTION: PLAN B*

Judith A. Johnson and Vanessa K. Burrows

SUMMARY

On August 24, 2006, the Food and Drug Administration (FDA) announced the approval of an application to switch Plan B, an emergency contraceptive, from a prescription-only drug to an over-the-counter (OTC) drug for women 18 years of age and older. Plan B will only be sold in pharmacies or healthcare clinics. It will continue to be dispensed as a prescription drug for women 17 years old and younger. Plan B is a brand of post-coital contraceptive that is administered within a few hours or days of unprotected intercourse. Emergency contraception prevents pregnancy; it does not disrupt an established pregnancy.

Approval of the switch to OTC status for Plan B has been controversial. Some Members of Congress urged the FDA to deny OTC status for Plan B. Individuals who criticize the three-year delay in deciding to switch to OTC believe that Bush Administration policy and FDA actions were based on political and ideological considerations rather than on sound science. Conservative religious and pro-life groups believe Plan B may increase unsafe sexual activity and should be used only under the supervision of a healthcare professional and, therefore, should not be available OTC. Their major concern

---

* This is an edited, reformatted and augmented version of a CRS Report for Congress publication, Report RL33728, dated August 1, 2007.

with Plan B, however, is that it might prevent the implantation of an embryo in the uterus, which to pro-life groups constitutes abortion. However, the medical community does not consider prevention of implantation to be an abortion, and FDA does not classify Plan B as an abortion drug.

Emergency contraceptives are currently available without a prescription in more than 40 countries. According to Barr Pharmaceuticals, sales of Plan B in the United States have doubled since August 2006, "rising from about $40 million a year to what will probably be close to $80 million for 2007." Women's health advocates claim that OTC status will improve access to the drug, thereby reducing the number of unintended pregnancies and reducing the number of abortions. However, a medical literature review, published in April 2007, found that "advance provision of emergency contraception did not reduce pregnancy rates when compared to conventional provision.... The interventions tested thus far have not reduced overall pregnancy rates in the populations studied."

The Office of Violence Against Women within the Department of Justice (DOJ) has developed guidelines for the treatment of sexual assault victims. The guidelines, released in September 2004, have been criticized by numerous organizations because they do not mention offering emergency contraception to female rape victims. In January 2005, a letter signed by 97 Members of Congress was sent to the Director of the Office on Violence Against Women expressing concern over the failure to mention emergency contraception and urging that the guidelines be changed to include such information.

Legislation introduced in the 110th Congress (S. 21/H.R. 819, H.R. 464, S. 1240, H.R. 2064/S. 1800, H.R. 2503, H.R. 2596/S. 1555) aims to ensure that Plan B is made available to women in general and sexual assault victims in particular or encourage education and provide information about Plan B.

INTRODUCTION

On August 24, 2006, the Food and Drug Administration (FDA) announced the approval of an application to switch Plan B, an emergency contraceptive, from a prescription-only drug to an over-the-counter (OTC) drug for women 18 years of age and older. Plan B will only be sold OTC in pharmacies or healthcare clinics. It will continue to be dispensed as a prescription drug for women 17 years old and younger. Both men and women will be able to purchase Plan B, but all individuals will need to show the pharmacist identification for proof of age before purchasing the OTC version.[1]

Anonymous shoppers will be used to test compliance with the age restriction. A booklet will be distributed with Plan B that explains proper use of the drug. The manufacturer, Barr Pharmaceuticals, began shipping the OTC version of the drug to U.S. pharmacies early in November 2006.[2]

Approval of the switch to OTC for Plan B has been controversial. Critics believe that initial policy decisions made by the Bush Administration regarding Plan B were based on political and ideological considerations rather than on sound science.[3] Conservative religious and pro-life groups believe that readily available Plan B may increase the occurrence of unsafe sexual activity and that such a drug should be used only under the supervision of a healthcare professional. Their primary concern with Plan B, however, is that it might prevent the implantation of the embryo in the uterus, which, for those who believe human life begins at conception, would constitute an abortion. However, the medical community does not consider prevention of implantation to be an abortion, and FDA does not classify Plan B as an abortion drug. Although the precise mechanism of action remains undetermined, scientific evidence suggests that prevention of ovulation or fertilization is the most likely mode of action for Plan B, rather than prevention of implantation of a developing embryo.[4]

This chapter discusses the FDA approval of Plan B as a prescription drug, as well as the more recent and controversial FDA approval of Plan B as an OTC drug. Legal issues regarding the recent FDA decision are also discussed as well as various state policies that affect access to emergency contraceptives. In addition, the report discusses the Department of Justice guidelines for the treatment of sexual assault victims, which have been criticized by numerous organizations because they do not mention offering emergency contraception to female rape victims. The DOJ guidelines were the focus of legislation introduced in the 109th Congress. Lastly, this chapter discusses the likely impact of the FDA Plan B OTC decision.

BACKGROUND INFORMATION ON EMERGENCY CONTRACEPTION

Emergency contraception is a therapy that may prevent pregnancy for women who have had unprotected sexual intercourse. There are two methods of emergency contraceptive therapy: insertion of an intrauterine devise, or IUD, within five days of intercourse; or, ingestion of a pill containing the hormones commonly found in the contraceptive pill. Although hormonal emergency contraception is often referred to as the "morning-after pill," it can be given up to 72 hours after unprotected intercourse and can involve taking more than one pill. Reasons for using emergency contraception include problems with a contraceptive (condom breakage, missed pill), sexual assault, or exposure to an agent which may cause a birth defect (e.g., live vaccine, cytotoxic drug, or radiation).

The current approach to emergency conception began with the recognition in the 1920s that estrogen prevented pregnancy in mammals. In the mid-1960s, a Dutch physician gave high-dose estrogen to a 13-year-old rape victim in order to prevent pregnancy. During the 1960s and 1970s high-dose estrogen became the standard emergency contraceptive treatment. In the early 1970s, Canadian physician A. Albert Yuzpe began studying emergency contraception and published his first study in 1974. The Yuzpe method used conventional birth control pills, a combination of estrogen and progestin, taken in two doses 12 hours apart.[5] In 1984, the United Kingdom became the first country to approve such a combination pill regimen as an emergency contraceptive.

In January 2001, the United Kingdom began allowing pharmacies to dispense emergency contraception without a prescription.[6] In April 2005, an emergency contraceptive (Plan B, a progestin-only pill) was approved by the Canadian government for use by all women without a prescription.[7] Emergency contraceptive pills are used by women in more than 100 countries; in over 40 countries the pills are sold without prescription either by a pharmacist or OTC (see **Table 1**, below).[8]

Table 1. Nonprescription Availability of Plan B

Over-the-counter
India, Netherlands, Norway, Sweden
Directly from a Pharmacist
Aruba, Australia, Belgium, Benin, Burkina Faso, Cameroon, Canada, China, Congo, Denmark, Estonia, Finland, France, French Polynesia, Gabon, Ghana, Greece, Guinea- Conakry, Iceland, Israel, Jamaica, Latvia, Libya, Luxembourg, Mali, Mauritania, Mauritius, New Zealand, Niger, Portugal, Senegal, Slovakia, South Africa, Sri Lanka, Switzerland, Togo, Tunisia, United Kingdom

FDA APPROVAL OF PREVEN AND PLAN B

Following the 1974 publication by Yuzpe, physicians often instructed patients to take multiple pills from a standard one-cycle oral contraceptive package for emergency contraception; this is referred to as an "off-label" use of the drug.[9] On February 25, 1997, a notice in the *Federal Register* stated that the Commissioner of FDA had concluded that certain oral contraceptives are safe and effective for use as emergency contraception and asked manufacturers to submit a new drug application for this use. In 1998, FDA approved Preven for use as an emergency contraceptive available by prescription. Preven utilized the Yuzpe method; two pills, containing estrogen and progestin, taken 12 hours apart.

A 1993 study conducted on about 800 women in Hong Kong found that use of progestin alone was somewhat more effective for emergency contraception than the Yuzpe method and had fewer side effects.[10] In 1998, the World Health Organization (WHO) followed up with a larger international trial using almost 2,000 women comparing the Yuzpe method and a progestin-only pill.[11] The WHO trial found that progestin alone was significantly more effective than the Yuzpe method at preventing pregnancy, and caused fewer side effects. **Most importantly, for either method, the WHO trial found that the earlier the pill is taken, the better it works.**

In the WHO trial, the progestin-alone regimen reduced the risk of pregnancy by 85% when taken within 72 hours of intercourse. Progestin prevented 95% of expected pregnancies when taken within 24 hours, 85% when taken between 25 and 48 hours, and 58% when taken between 49 and 72 hours. In contrast, Yuzpe reduced the risk of pregnancy by 57% when taken within 72 hours. Yuzpe prevented 77% of expected pregnancies when taken within 24 hours, 36% for 25 to 48 hours, and 31% for 49 to 72 hours. WHO also found that the Yuzpe method resulted in significantly more side effects than progestin alone. The incidence of nausea was 50% with Yuzpe and 23% with progestin. Vomiting with Yuzpe was 3 times higher than with progestin (19% vs. 6%), which is significant as women who vomit after taking the first combination pill may need to take an extra dose.[12]

On July 28, 1999, FDA approved Plan B, a progestin-only emergency contraceptive, for use by prescription. Plan B consists of two pills each containing 0.75 mg of levonorgestrel (a progestin).[13] One pill is taken as soon as possible after unprotected intercourse and the second is taken 12 hours later.[14] The FDA-approved labeling for Plan B states that it is 89% effective if taken within three days (72 hours) after unprotected sex. In other words, 7 of every 8 women who would have become pregnant will not become pregnant. As mentioned earlier, Plan B is even more effective (95%) if taken within 24 hours of unprotected sex.

Mechanism of Action

In humans, the fertile days when sexual intercourse can result in pregnancy include the five days before ovulation (release of the egg from the ovary) and the day of ovulation. Although the precise mechanism of action by which Plan B prevents pregnancy remains undetermined, scientific evidence suggests that prevention of ovulation or fertilization is the most likely mode of action for Plan B, rather than prevention of implantation.[15] The active ingredient in Plan B, levonorgestrel, has been used in birth control pills for more than 35 years. Emergency contraception is not as effective as the regular use of oral contraceptives. However, the higher dose of levonorgestrel in Plan B works like a birth control pill to prevent pregnancy, most probably by stopping ovulation. Several studies indicate that hormonal emergency contraception interferes with the events in the ovary that lead up to release of the egg.[16]

Plan B may also interfere with fertilization by altering the transport of sperm and/or egg within the female reproductive system. In one study, administration of levonorgestrel after sexual intercourse reduced the number of sperm within the uterus, increased the pH of the uterine fluid (which immobilized sperm), and increased the viscosity of cervical mucus (which impeded entry of sperm into the uterus).[17]

It is possible that Plan B may inhibit implantation of the fertilized egg within the uterus by altering the endometrium (the uterine lining). Three studies of hormonal emergency contraception in human subjects found alterations in the endometrium, but whether such changes had an impact on implantation was "open to question."[18] Four other studies found either negligible or no alterations in the endometrium. However, in the case of levonorgestrel, "publications in refereed journals do not support the hypothesis that it alters endometrial receptivity or impedes implantation."[19] In addition, studies in the rat and monkey indicate that levonorgestrel does not disrupt post-fertilization events such as implantation.[20]

Plan B is not effective after the embryo has implanted in the uterus and therefore cannot interfere with an established pregnancy, which is defined as an embryo implanted in a uterus. Plan B is used before a pregnancy can be diagnosed. Plan B does not use the same active ingredient as Mifeprex (also known as the abortion pill, RU-486, or mifepristone). Mifeprex (in combination with misoprostol) is used after a positive pregnancy test to terminate an early pregnancy (up through seven weeks).[21]

Contraindications and Adverse Reactions

The fact that there are relatively few side effects for Plan B was a major factor in the approval of OTC status for this drug. The FDA-approved OTC labeling lists known pregnancy and hypersensitivity to any component of the product as contraindications. For Preven or the Yuzpe regimen, the FDA, WHO, and the American College of Obstetricians and Gynecologists (ACOG) list known pregnancy as the only contraindication. (Pregnancy is listed as a contraindication only because these drugs won't work to prevent pregnancy if the patient is already pregnant; no harm will result if a pregnant patient takes either pill.) The FDA, however, lists some relative contraindications based on evidence from combination estrogen-progestin oral contraceptives. These include clotting problems, stroke, and migraine, among others, which are related to the presence of estrogen in the combination pill. A 1997 review found that since the Yuzpe regimen was approved in 1984 in the UK, the product was used more than 4 million times; only six serious stroke or blood clot events were reported, and there was no clear-cut relationship between drug administration and any of these events.[22] In contrast, such events are much more likely during pregnancy (60 cases/100,000 women). Without the presence of estrogen, the incidence of such events for use of Plan B should be even lower than the Yuzpe regimen.

Adverse reactions to Plan B listed in the FDA-approved label include nausea (23%), abdominal pain (18%), fatigue (17%), and headache (17%). Less common adverse events listed on the label include menstrual changes, dizziness, breast tenderness, vomiting, and diarrhea. There is no medical evidence that Plan B will harm a developing fetus if taken accidentally while pregnant.[23] Several studies have shown that availability of Plan B does not lead to an increase in unprotected sex.[24]

FDA APPROVAL OF OVER-THE-COUNTER STATUS FOR PLAN B

In April 2003, Women's Capital Corporation (WCC) submitted an application to the FDA requesting that Plan B be switched from prescription to OTC.[25] Requiring a prescription for emergency contraception may create barriers to access for many women. The woman must: (1) identify a physician who will prescribe Plan B; (2) obtain a prescription via a telephone call or a physician visit and pay the financial cost of the visit; and, (3) find a pharmacy that stocks the product and employs a pharmacist who will dispense the product. Because the effective use of Plan B is time dependent (the earlier it is used, the more effective it is), a switch from "prescription only" to "over-the-counter" (OTC) would likely benefit women who may need to use this product.

FDA formalized the process of switching a prescription drug to OTC status in 1975 and has approved over 90 such applications. The requirements for making the switch from prescription-only to OTC include making sure the drug is safe for selfmedication and has a low toxicity or other potentiality for harmful effect.[26] The patient must be able to recognize the condition and require minimal health care provider intervention in order to use the drug correctly. The OTC applications are reviewed by FDA's Center for Drug Evaluation and Research (CDER). Because it is considered to be a "first in class" drug, the Plan B application was reviewed by two (rather than one) of the six offices within CDER, one office with expertise in reproductive health and a second office that reviews all OTC switch applications.

CDER also requested a joint meeting of two advisory committees of outside experts in order to obtain scientific advice on the Plan B application. The two committees, the Nonprescription Drugs Advisory Committee and the Advisory Committee for Reproductive Health Drugs, met in December 2003.[27] After reviewing over 15,000 pages of data and 40 scientific studies, the committees voted unanimously that Plan B is safe for use in the nonprescription setting, and voted 23 to 4 that the Plan B switch to OTC status should be approved.[28]

In May 2004 the FDA rejected the advice of its scientific committee and issued a "not-approvable" letter for the Plan B switch to OTC. The FDA cited "inadequate sampling" of women under 16 years of age as the reason for the rejection and concerns about use of the drug without supervision by a physician or other health care provider. However, studies published in 2004 and 2005 do not support an association between wider availability of emergency contraception and an increase in unsafe sexual behavior among teenagers.[29] Counseling against unsafe behavior in this age group is presumably the reason why FDA believed the supervision of a physician was required.

Barr Labs reapplied in July 2004, requesting that Plan B be available over the counter only to women 17 years and older. The FDA did not issue a decision by its regulatory deadline of January 2005. At his confirmation hearing in March 2005, FDA Commissioner Lester M. Crawford indicated that "the science part is generally done" for the Plan B approval process, and "we're just now down to what the label will look like."[30]

FDA announced on August 26, 2005, that an immediate decision on the OTC switch could not be determined. FDA Commissioner Lester Crawford cited "novel regulatory issues," "profound" policy questions, and specific concerns over how the exact same formulation of the drug could be available OTC for an older group of women while remaining prescription only for the younger group. A 60-day "public comment" period was opened to help decide these issues. This announcement led to the resignation on August 31 of the director of the FDA's Office of Women's Health, Susan Wood, in protest of the agency's action. FDA Commissioner Crawford resigned abruptly on September 23, 2005, reportedly due to financial improprieties unrelated to the ongoing controversy over Plan B.

When the comment period ended on November 1, 2005, FDA had received approximately 47,000 comments.[31] On that same day Senators Hillary Clinton and Patty Murray delivered a 10,000-name petition urging the agency to "expeditiously make a decision on the application for OTC status for Plan B based strictly on scientific evidence."[32]

Members of Congress asked the Government Accountability Office (GAO) to investigate if there was political interference in the FDA decision process. The GAO report, released in November 2005, stated that the process was "unusual" and that the decision may have been made months before the scientific reviews were completed. It noted that it was "not typical of the other 67 proposed prescription-to-OTC switch decisions made from 1994 through 2004" for two reasons. First, it was the only decision that was not approved after the members of the advisory committees voted to approve the application. Second, the GAO reported that three high-level FDA officials had declined to sign the letter that refused approval. "This action removed decision-making authority from the directors of the reviewing offices who would normally make the decision," stated the GAO. The GAO urged Health and Human Services Secretary Mike Leavitt to assure that an upcoming decision about the pill's status "is based on the best available science instead of ideology."

In July 2006, FDA stated that it had evaluated the public comments and decided that it could proceed without creating a new regulation to allow the drug to be offered without a prescription to adults. Barr resubmitted its OTC application to FDA in mid-August 2006 and FDA approved the switch to OTC on August 24, 2006. The manufacturer agreed to the use of anonymous shoppers to test compliance with the age restriction. Barr also agreed that a booklet will be distributed with the drug that explains proper use of the drug. The age restriction was changed from 17 to 18 because it is the "age of majority" and sales of nicotine replacement treatments (gum and patch) are allowed at 18 years of age.[33] In approving nicotine replacement treatments for OTC sales, FDA also restricted sales to individuals 18 and over.

LEGAL ISSUES[34]

At least three lawsuits have been filed with regard to the FDA's approval of Plan B, or the approval process itself. In *Tummino v. von Eschenbach,*[35] representatives of several reproductive health organizations filed a complaint against FDA Commissioner Andrew von Eschenbach, on behalf of women seeking emergency contraception. The suit was filed on January 21, 2005, over a year and a half before the FDA announced its approval of the OTC switch for Plan B for women 18 and older.[36] The case has yet to go to trial. In light of the FDA's bifurcated approval, the plaintiffs amended their filing and asked the court to require the FDA to approve Plan B for all ages, remove the agency's requirement that pharmacists keep Plan B behind the counter, and allow all businesses to sell Plan B.[37]

The plaintiffs, some as young as 13, argue that the FDA did not follow proper agency procedures when it mandated age and point-of-sale restrictions for Plan B.[38] Because the drug is used only by women, they contend that the FDA engaged in sex discrimination in violation of the Fifth Amendment right to Equal Protection. The plaintiffs also assert that the agency violated their Fifth Amendment right to privacy "without serving any compelling, significant, or even legitimate government interest" by restricting access to certain ages, the location of the drug behind the counter, and sales in certain businesses.[39] Next, the plaintiffs object to alleged violations of the right to informational privacy that will occur because they must disclose their ages and possibly other information, such as names and addresses, to obtain Plan B from behind the counter. The plaintiffs view this as a "disclosure of information to third parties about [their] personal sexual activity."[40] Finally, the plaintiffs contend that the agency ignored certain requirements under the Administrative Procedure Act (APA).[41]

With regard to the alleged APA violations, the plaintiffs specifically argue that the agency's imposition of age and point-of-sale restrictions was arbitrary, capricious, and an abuse of agency discretion. The FDA allegedly required greater information for the approval of Plan B than the agency required for past approvals of OTC medications.[42] Additionally, the plaintiffs argue that the FDA had enough data regarding Plan B's safety and effectiveness to make the drug available OTC without further restrictions.[43] The plaintiffs also contend that the agency took improper action when determining age restrictions for Plan B, despite recommendations within the agency that the FDA approve Plan B without age limits.[44] According to the lawsuit, the FDA also violated the APA by overstepping its statutory mandate in two ways. First, the FDA's denial was purportedly influenced by logic other than scientific or medical evidence:

> Sworn depositions taken by lawyers from the Center for Reproductive Rights, a legal advocacy organization, show that some of the [FDA]'s staff members were convinced that no amount of scientific evidence would have persuaded the [FDA]'s political appointees to approve the application. Dr. John Jenkins, director of the Office of New Drugs at the agency, said in a deposition that his boss, Dr. Steven Galson, told him "that he felt he didn't have a choice" but to reject the application.[45]

Second, the plaintiffs assert that "the FDA lack[ed] the statutory authority to restrict the types of businesses that can sell OTC drugs," and the "authority to control the point of sale of nonprescription drug products."[46]

In response to the amended complaint, the FDA moved to dismiss the case on the grounds that (1) the court lacks jurisdiction, (2) the plaintiffs do not have standing to bring the case, (3) the complaint's allegations fail to state a claim for which the court may grant relief, (4) the plaintiffs' claims are moot, and (5) the court lacks the authority to grant the requested relief.[47]

Furthermore, the FDA acknowledged that it has received at least four citizens petitions on Plan B and denied at least one.[48] The FDA also admitted that, for the ten years prior, the agency either approved applications for OTC status after its advisory committee recommended granting the applicant OTC status, or the agency did not reach a final determination on the application.[49]

The FDA said that in those ten years, it requested subsequent information on teen use not only for Plan B, but also for OTC nicotine replacement therapies, and noted that several past supplemental new drug applications included information on teen use of prescription drugs when requesting OTC status.[50] In addition, the FDA specifically denied that it created a behind-the-counter "regime" for Plan B and that the FDA mandated that it be kept behind-the-counter.[51]

In response to the plaintiffs' suggestions that the FDA's Plan B review procedures were politicized and unusual, the agency initially claimed that privilege protected it from discussing its deliberative process, including advice, opinions, and ideas received by the agency and presented by those involved in the process.[52] In an amended answer, the FDA later stated that such allegations were irrelevant and immaterial to the complaint's causes of action, as well as beyond the court's jurisdiction.[53] Notably, scientific data reviewed by the FDA's Center for Drug Evaluation and Research determined that Plan B could be safely used by women age 17 and older.[54]

As noted above, the suit was filed before the FDA approved the application to switch Plan B to OTC status for women ages 18 and older, but the plaintiffs are currently pursuing the case with respect to women younger than 18. Most recently, the plaintiffs have asked for summary judgment, a request made because, allegedly, no material issues of fact exist and thus the plaintiffs are entitled to a judgment in their favor.

In *Judicial Watch, Inc. v. FDA*,[55] the conservative non-profit sued the FDA for violating the Freedom of Information Act with regard to the agency's communications with Members of Congress about Plan B. The relevant provision of that Act requires that the agency, upon receiving a request for records, decide whether it will comply with such request within 20 business days after receiving such request.[56] Judicial Watch had requested records of any and all communications between the FDA and Senators Clinton, Murray, and Enzi and their staff members with regard to Plan B. The FDA filed a motion to dismiss, noting that it had "produced all responsive records,"[57] which the agency argued renders the case moot because "it gives the requester the relief sought in the FOIA complaint."[58] Alternatively, the FDA moved for summary judgment on the issue of the adequacy of the agency's records of its communications with the Senators and their staff members, asserting that its search was adequate and "reasonable as a matter of law."[59] These motions are pending before the federal district court for D.C.

In *Association of American Physicians & Surgeons, Inc. v. FDA*,[60] a not-for-profit organization representing physicians in typically small or solo practices and three conservative women's and reproductive health groups filed suit seeking to overturn the FDA's approval of Plan B as an OTC drug so that the drug would become available, again, only by prescription. First, the plaintiffs argue that Plan B is unsafe for OTC distribution because the label "does not adequately warn consumers of Plan B's ineffectiveness for routine contraception" and because information submitted to the FDA in support of the change to an OTC drug did not "establish either Plan B's safety or effectiveness."[61] Second, the plaintiffs allege that the FDA lacked the authority to approve a drug both OTC and as a prescription because the Federal Food, Drug, and Cosmetic Act (FFDCA) does not authorize approval or distribution of the same drug for sale both OTC and as a prescription. Third, citing the FDA's inability to enforce age restrictions and alleged errors in waiving pediatric research requirements, the complaint asserts that the FDA could not lawfully "bifurcate a drug product's OTC versus Rx status based on the patient's age," under the FFDCA.[62] Fourth, the plaintiffs assert that the FDA does not have the power to create a new, third class of drugs, those "that require pharmacists to supplement the labeling or that certain subpopulations might misuse with direct access."[63] Next, the plaintiffs assert that the FDA did not engage in the necessary rulemaking under the APA when amending its interpretation of a statutory provision to approve Plan B as an OTC drug.[64] In addition, the plaintiffs allege that the FDA did not follow the FFDCA when it removed Plan B from prescription status without a rulemaking.[65] Finally, they argue that the FDA unlawfully approved Plan B as an OTC drug "under improper pressure from Senators Clinton and Murray."[66] As a result, according to the plaintiffs, the FDA's approval of Plan B and the agency's avoidance of the rulemaking process was arbitrary and capricious.

In response, the FDA moved to dismiss the suit on five grounds: (1) the plaintiffs lack standing to challenge the FDA's approval decision of Plan B's supplemental new drug application, (2) the court lacks subject matter jurisdiction to review the FDA's approval of the Plan B supplemental new drug application, (3) the plaintiffs failed to state a claim as far as their allegations that the FDA lacked the authority to approve Plan B both OTC and as a prescription drug and that the FDA did not have the power to create a third class of behind-the-counter drugs, (4) the plaintiffs' contentions that the FDA violated the APA and the FFDCA by failing to engage in a rulemaking were incorrect as a matter of law, and (5) FDA Commissioner Von Eschenbach was improperly named as a defendant in his individual capacity because the plaintiffs' claims related to official FDA actions.[67] The case has yet to go to trial.

STATE POLICIES[68]

About half the states have adopted policies that affect access to emergency contraceptives. Several states have passed pharmacy access laws that allow women to obtain emergency contraception directly from a pharmacy without first going to a doctor or clinic.[69] With the FDA's decision, these measures will now apply only to minors.[70] Plan B is available from pharmacists, without a physician's prescription, under certain conditions in the following nine states: Alaska, California, Hawaii, Maine, Massachusetts, New Hampshire, New Mexico, Vermont, and Washington.[71] In these states, pharmacists are allowed to sell emergency contraception to women who ask for the product. After speaking with the woman, the pharmacist determines if emergency contraception is appropriate. In order to participate, the pharmacy and the pharmacist must fill out application forms and undergo training. Access is still limited in these states by the number of pharmacies that participate.

Several states have laws that specifically pertain to emergency room practices with respect to emergency contraceptives. For example, in seven states — California, Massachusetts, New Jersey, New Mexico, New York, South Carolina, and Washington — hospital emergency rooms must dispense emergency contraceptives upon request to sexual assault victims; similar policies in Ohio and Oregon do not have an enforcement mechanism. In May 2007, Governor Jodi Rell signed into law a measure that requires all hospitals in Connecticut, including Catholic hospitals, to provide emergency contraception to rape victims; the law takes effect on October 1 2007.[72] Emergency rooms must provide information about emergency contraceptives in 10 states: Arkansas, California, Colorado, Illinois, Massachusetts, New Jersey, New Mexico, New York, Texas, and Washington. A similar policy in Ohio does not have an enforcement mechanism.

Several states have enacted laws regarding pharmacists who refuse to dispense birth control and emergency contraception.[73] These laws vary widely from state to state. Four states (Arkansas, Georgia, Mississippi, and South Dakota) explicitly allow pharmacists to refuse to dispense contraceptives, including emergency contraceptives. In five states (Colorado, Florida, Illinois, Maine, and Tennessee), a broadly worded refusal policy may apply to pharmacists or pharmacies, but does not specifically include them. In Illinois, however, pharmacies that stock contraceptives must also dispense emergency contraceptives. In the state of Washington, a recent rulemaking by the state's Board of Pharmacy requires pharmacy owners to ensure that if one pharmacist refuses to fill a prescription, another pharmacist will deliver the lawfully prescribed drug or device to the patient.[74] If a prescription drug or device is out-of-stock, the new rule provides several options to the patient, including transmitting the patient's prescription to another pharmacy, chosen by the patient, that will fill the prescription.[75] The Washington State regulations are being challenged in federal district court by the parent corporation of two grocery stores, including one that has a pharmacy, and two pharmacists who are the sole pharmacists on duty at pharmacies that allegedly could not hire another pharmacist to dispense drugs such as Plan B.[76]

On March 20, 2006, all Wal-Mart pharmacies began stocking and filling prescriptions for Plan B. Prior to that date, the company only stocked and filled prescriptions for the drug at its pharmacies in Massachusetts and Illinois where it was required by law. The company decided to change its policy because Wal-Mart expects more states to require Plan B to be available for sale. "Because of this, and the fact that [Plan B] is an FDA-approved product, we feel it is difficult to justify being the country's only major pharmacy chain not selling it."[77] The company intends to keep its "conscientious objection" policy, which allows pharmacists to refuse to fill prescriptions and refer patients to another pharmacy or pharmacist. There are more than 3,700 Wal-Mart pharmacies nationwide.

Connecticut Attorney General Richard Blumenthal announced on March 4, 2006, that state health plans would not cover prescriptions from pharmacies that do not stock Plan B. Attorney General Blumenthal said that his decision to remove pharmacies from the state's health plan coverage would remain until he is certain "every pharmacy will dispense [Plan B] wherever it is medically prescribed."[78]

There is great variation among the states regarding emergency contraception coverage for Medicaid beneficiaries.[79] Following the August 2006 FDA decision, 16 states have implemented written policies to address coverage of emergency contraception as an OTC drug. Most of the remaining states had policies on emergency contraception coverage prior to August 2006, and those policies remain in effect. Because the billing procedures of most state Medicaid programs require the pharmacist to submit a prescription in order to be reimbursed for OTC drugs, low-income women must either obtain a prescription or pay the $40 out-of-pocket cost. In nine states (Alabama, Arizona, Idaho, Indiana, Kentucky, Maryland, Nevada, North Carolina, Rhode Island) prior authorization is required for emergency contraception reimbursement. The dual status of Plan B (OTC for women 18 and over, prescription-only for women under 18) is creating coverage disparities.

For example, the Georgia Medicaid program, which allows very limited coverage for OTC drugs, has revised its provider manual to exclude coverage of Plan B for women 18 and older while covering the drug for women 17 and under who have a doctor's prescription. Arkansas will cover two tablets per prescription. In other states, such as North Carolina, Medicaid will cover [emergency contraception] for women only if they have a doctor's prescription for the drug, regardless of their age.[80]

In Hawaii, Illinois, Maryland, New Jersey, New York, Oklahoma, Oregon, and Washington, Medicaid will cover Plan B as an OTC drug for women over age 18 without the need for a prescription.[81] Mississippi, however, has decided to exclude emergency contraception from Medicaid coverage.[82]

JUSTICE DEPARTMENT GUIDELINES FOR SEXUAL ASSAULT VICTIMS

The National Violence Against Women Survey, which was conducted in 1996 and 1997, found that an estimated 300,000 women were raped in a single year.[83] Based on an estimated 333,000 rapes occurring in 1998, as many as 25,000 pregnancies resulted due to rape in that year; potentially 22,000 of such pregnancies could have been prevented if women had been provided with emergency contraceptive treatment.[84]

The Office of Violence Against Women within the Department of Justice (DOJ) developed guidelines for the treatment of sexual assault victims pursuant to Section 1405 of the Violence against Women Act of 2000 (P.L. 106-386). The guidelines serve as an informational resource to communities as they develop or revise their own procedures and do not invalidate any jurisdictional protocols, policies or practices. Released in September 2004, the 141 page document, *A National Protocol for Sexual Assault Medical Forensic Examination*,[85] has been criticized by numerous organizations because it does not mention offering emergency contraception to female rape victims.

The DOJ *Protocol* states on page 111: "Patients of different ages, social, cultural, and religious/spiritual backgrounds may have varying feelings regarding acceptable treatment options. Examiners and other involved health care personnel must be careful not to influence patients' choices of treatment." The DOJ *Protocol* recommends that health care providers: discuss the probability of pregnancy with female patients; conduct a pregnancy test for all patients with reproductive capability (with their consent); and discuss treatment options with patients. A footnote directs the reader to the National Sexual Violence Resource Center (877-739-3895 or 717- 909-0710 or [http://www.nsvrc.org].) for more detailed information about sexual assault and pregnancy. An early draft of the document did include mention of emergency contraception.[86] In contrast to the half page of information on pregnancy, the *Protocol* offers several pages of information on treatment of sexually transmitted diseases.

The American College of Obstetricians and Gynecologists and the American Public Health Association recommend that emergency contraception should be offered to female rape victims who are at risk of pregnancy.[87] The American Medical Association, the American Nurses Association, the American College of Emergency Physicians, the American Academy of Pediatrics, and the Society for Adolescent Medicine also support advising rape victims about emergency contraception and providing the drug when appropriate.[88]

A letter signed by 277 national, state, and local organizations and individuals was sent to the Department of Justice on January 6, 2005, strongly urging that the *Protocol* be amended to include the routine offering of emergency contraception to sexual assault victims who are at risk of pregnancy.[89] According to the letter, hospitals often do not provide this service: only 6% of hospitals in Louisiana, 8% of hospitals in Idaho and 20% of hospitals in Montana provide emergency contraception on-site to rape victims.

On January 13, 2005, a letter signed by 97 Members of Congress was sent to the Director of the Office on Violence Against Women expressing concern over the failure to mention emergency contraception and urging that the Protocol be changed to include such information.[90]

FEDERAL LEGISLATION

S. 21 (Reid), the Prevention First Act, was introduced on January 4, 2007. The bill would expand access to preventive health care services that help reduce unintended pregnancy, reduce abortions, and improve access to women's health care. It directs the Secretary of Health and Human Services (HHS) to develop and disseminate information on emergency contraception to the public and to health care providers. S. 21 would require hospitals, as a condition of receiving federal funds, to offer and to provide, upon request, emergency contraception to victims of sexual assault. S. 21 was referred to the

Senate Health, Education, Labor, and Pensions Committee. S. 21 is similar to S. 20 (Reid), which was introduced in the 109th Congress. A companion bill, H.R. 819 (Slaughter), was introduced in the House on February 5, 2007.

H.R. 464 (Rothman), the Compassionate Assistance for Rape Emergencies Act of 2007, was introduced on January 12, 2007. H.R. 464 is similar to H.R. 2928 (Rothman), which was introduced in the 109th Congress. The bill would prohibit any federal funds from being provided to a hospital under Medicare or to a state, with respect to hospital services, under Medicaid, unless certain conditions are met. A woman who is a victim of sexual assault must be provided with (1) accurate and unbiased information about emergency contraception, (2) an offer of emergency contraception, (3) emergency contraception must be provided to the woman upon her request, and (4) such services cannot be denied because of the inability to pay. H.R. 464 was referred to the Committee on Energy and Commerce and the Committee on Ways and Means. S. 1240 (Clinton), introduced on April 26, 2007, has the same language and title as H.R. 464, but it would also provide a woman with risk assessment, counseling, and treatment for certain sexually transmitted infections. S. 1240 was referred to the Committee on Finance.

H.R. 2064 (Michaud), the Compassionate Care for Servicewomen Act, was introduced on April 26, 2007. The bill would require emergency contraception to be included on the basic core formulary of the uniform formulary of pharmaceutical agents for the pharmacy benefits program of the Department of Defense. Under the bill, prior authorization would not be required for emergency contraception. H.R. 2064 was referred to the Subcommittee on Military Personnel. A companion bill, S. 1800 (Clinton), was introduced on July 17, 2007. S. 1800 was referred to the Committee on Armed Services.

H.R. 2503 (DeLauro), the FDA Scientific Fairness for Women Act, was introduced on May 24, 2007. Among other things, the bill would provide for a scientific workshop to review and evaluate current scientific data on the use of emergency contraceptives by women under the age of 18. The bill was referred to the House Committee on Energy and Commerce.

H.R. 2596 (Maloney)/S. 1555 (Lautenberg), the Access to Birth Control Act, was introduced on June 6, 2007. The bill would amend Title II of the Public Health Service Act establishing certain duties for pharmacies to ensure the provision of an FDA-approved contraceptive, including an emergency contraceptive, to a customer requesting such a product. The bill would provide a civil penalty for a violation of up to $5,000 per day, not to exceed $500,000 for all violations adjudicated in a single proceeding. H.R. 2596 was referred to the House Committee on Energy and Commerce; S. 1555 was referred to the Committee on Health, Education, Labor, and Pensions.

IMPACT OF THE FDA OTC DECISION

The Plan B OTC application was mired in controversy over the three year period from when it was filed with FDA in April 2003 to its August 2006 approval. Individuals who criticize the delayed FDA decision believe that Bush Administration policy and FDA actions were based on political and ideological considerations rather than on sound science. FDA is required by law to make decisions exclusively on substantial scientific evidence regarding the safety and efficacy of a drug. These critics believe the FDA decision was delayed to appease conservative religious and pro-life groups that are long time supporters of President Bush.

President Bush indicated his support for the then-imminent Plan B decision during a news conference on August 21, 2006.[91] The FDA decision and the President's support of the decision have greatly angered conservative religious and pro-life groups. One such organization, Concerned Women of America, asked that Dr. Andrew von Eschenbach's nomination as FDA commissioner be withdrawn and recommended that consumers stop doing business with drug stores that sell OTC Plan B.[92] The Family Research Council, a Christian conservative non-profit think tank and lobbying organization, states that it is "pursuing legal and legislative options" to overturn the FDA's decision.[93] Such groups are unhappy because they believe Plan B should only be used with the supervision of a healthcare professional; they also believe Plan B use may lead to an increase in unsafe sexual activity.

A recent review of the medical literature, published in April 2007, found that having emergency contraception on hand "did not lead to increased rates of sexually transmitted infections, increased frequency of unprotected intercourse, nor changes in contraceptive methods."[94] A U.S. study also found that easier access to emergency contraception did not decrease the use of condoms or oral contraceptives or lead to an increase in sexually transmitted infections or unprotected sex.[95] A followup study found that adolescents younger than 16 years of age behaved no differently in response to increased access to emergency contraception compared with older age groups.[96] Their behaviors did not become riskier: no increased incidence of unprotected sex, sexually transmitted disease, or pregnancy, nor did they become more vulnerable to unwanted sexual activity, including the very youngest participants in the study. Moreover, "the adolescents were equally capable as adults in taking EC correctly, with the youngest adolescents, under 16 years, showing the best results. These results are consistent with findings from [a] previous study that specifically examined young adolescents ... there was no reason to restrict access in this age group. The high levels of correct use ... in this study suggest that physician supervision does not improve adherence to the regimen and that young adolescents should not be singled out due to concerns about their inability to follow the regimen correctly."[97]

The Society for Adolescent Medicine does not place an age limit on access to emergency contraception.[98] The American College of Obstetricians and Gynecologists (ACOG) believes that Plan B can be safely used without supervision by a physician, and that the age restriction imposed by FDA is medically unnecessary. In a statement released on the same day as the FDA approval of OTC status for Plan B, ACOG stated:

> By restricting its OTC availability to women age 18 and older, the FDA has missed an unparalleled opportunity to prevent teenage pregnancies. Each year there are more than 800,000 teen pregnancies in the US, with many ending in abortion. Pregnancy itself is not without risk, especially for a young woman. There is no scientific or medical reason to impose an age restriction and to withhold emergency contraception from this population. Emergency contraception is safe for over-the-counter use by women of all ages.[99]

As stated above, studies of Plan B have shown that women, even young adolescents, can follow the directions on the package and use the product correctly without an increase in high risk behaviors.[100] One member of the FDA advisory panel, a pharmacist, noted that for even the youngest women, the morning-after pill poses less of a health risk than pregnancy: "In terms of age, I'm not an OB-GYN, but I can't imagine that I would prefer a ten or 11 year old to be pregnant over some hypothetical risk that there might be with a ten or 11 year old taking this product. So I guess I would feel pretty strongly about not having any age restrictions."[101] The side effects of Plan B would probably influence most women to find another method of regular birth control. For rape victims who don't immediately seek medical care, OTC availability would be expected to be beneficial. Under the FDA approval agreement with Barr, the drug will only be sold in pharmacies or health clinics where consumers can obtain advice from a pharmacist or other health care professional. Plan B will not be available at gas stations, convenience stores, online pharmacies, or other places where other nonprescription drugs are sold.

The primary concern of conservative religious and pro-life groups with Plan B, however, is that it may prevent the implantation of the embryo in the uterus. Pro-life groups believe that prevention of embryo implantation in the uterus is an abortion. According to the Catholic pro-life group Human Life International, "President Bush's implied support for the abortion-causing drug Plan B is completely inconsistent with his recent veto of the embryonic stem cell research (ESCR) funding bill. What the president apparently fails to realize is that Plan B kills the same innocent unborn children that the ESCR process does."[102] The medical community, however, does not consider prevention of implantation to be an abortion. "Pregnancy begins with implantation, not fertilization. Medical organizations and the federal government concur on this point. Fertilization is a necessary but insufficient step toward pregnancy.... Any method of regulation of fertility that acts before implantation is not an abortifacient."[103] FDA does not classify Plan B as an abortion drug.

Research has found that the use of emergency contraception rises when it is made available without a prescription. In France, sales of a nonprescription emergency contraceptive, introduced in 1999, rose 72% over five years.[104] In British Columbia, use of emergency contraception increased 102% after a new policy allowed pharmacists to dispense without a prescription.[105] Some experts have estimated that use of emergency contraception in the United States could prevent 1 million abortions and more than 2 million unintended pregnancies that result in childbirth each year.[106] However, a report in the January 2007 issue of Obstetrics & Gynecology, which looked at 23 studies of emergency contraception use, found that "increased access to emergency contraceptive pills enhances use but has not been shown to reduce unintended pregnancy rates."[107] This same conclusion was reached in a separate review of the medical literature published in April 2007.[108] The authors of this second study found that "advance provision of emergency contraception did not reduce pregnancy rates when compared to conventional provision.... The interventions tested thus far have not reduced overall pregnancy rates in the populations studied."[109]

Pro-choice groups believe OTC status for Plan B will reduce the number of unintended pregnancies and reduce the number of abortions performed in the United States. Although pro-choice groups believe the FDA decision is a step in the right direction, they would have preferred that OTC status for Plan B would have been approved for all women, not just those 18 and older. They believe that the age restriction might keep the drug from women who need it the most. An estimated 3.5 million unwanted pregnancies occur annually, one third of which involve teenagers.[110] In the United States, four in ten girls become pregnant at least once before turning 20.[111]

Prescriptions of Plan B have been covered by most state Medicaid programs and many private health insurers.[112] Drugs that are switched to OTC typically lose insurance coverage and therefore the OTC switch for Plan B may result in increased cost to insured consumers who buy the drug without a prescription. Prior to the change to OTC status, Plan B was prescribed about 1.5 million times per year in the United States; about half are filled in clinics such as Planned Parenthood or on college campuses.[113] During its first month as an OTC drug, Plan B was available in in one state, Pennsylvania for $20 through Planned Parenthood clinics and for $39.99 to $44.99 at various retail pharmacies.[114] According to Barr Pharmaceuticals, sales of Plan B in the United States have doubled since August 2006, "rising from about $40 million a year to what will probably be close to $80 million for 2007."[115]

End Notes

[1] See the FDA approved label for Plan B (levonorgestrel) at [http://www.fda.gov/cder/foi/label/2006/021045s011lbl.pdf], and, Joyce Howard Price, "Plan B Allowed Over The Counter," *The Washington Times*, August 25, 2006.

[2] Stacy Forster, "Now, consumers weigh in on Plan B debate: Over-the-counter sales of contraceptive begin," *The Milwaukee Journal Sentinel*, November 20, 2006, p. A1.

[3] Jeffrey M. Drazen et al., "The FDA, Politics, and Plan B," *The New England Journal of Medicine*, v. 350, April 8, 2004, pp. 1561-1562.

[4] Horacio B. Croxatto et al., "Mechanisms of Action of Emergency Contraception," *Steroids*, v. 68, 2003, pp. 1095-1098.

[5] Progestin is a synthetic form of the hormone progesterone.

[6] Haroon Ashraf and Michael McCarthy, "UK Improves Access to Morning After Pill," *The Lancet*, December 16, 2000, p. 2071.

[7] "Health Canada Gives Canadian Women a Plan B," *Canada NewsWire*, April 20, 2005, p. 1.

[8] NOT-2-LATE.com The Emergency Contraception Website [http://ec.princeton.edu/questions/dedicated.html].

[9] Off-label use is defined as "use for an indication, dosage form, dose regimen, population or other use parameter not mentioned in the approved labeling." Found at [http://www.fda.gov/cder/present/diamontreal/regappr/sld003.htm]. FDA does not regulate the practice of medicine; section 906 [21 U.S.C. 396] of the Food, Drug & Cosmetic Act states "Nothing in this Act shall be construed to limit or interfere with the authority of a health care practitioner to prescribe or administer any legally marketed device to a patient for any condition or disease within a legitimate health care practitioner-patient relationship."

[10] P.C. Ho and M.S.W. Kwan, "A prospective randomized comparison of levonorgestrel with the Yuzpe regimen in post-coital contraception," *Human Reproduction*, v. 8, 1993, pp. 389-392.

[11] Task Force on Postovulatory Methods of Fertility Regulation, "Randomized Controlled Trial of Levenorgestrel Versus the Yuzpe Regimen of Combined Oral Contraceptives for Emergency Contraception," *Lancet*, v. 352, August 8, 1998, pp. 428-433.

[12] The manufacturer of Preven elected to discontinue making the product in 2004, probably because of the difference in side effects. Planned Parenthood, A Brief History of Emergency Hormonal Contraception, September 2005 [http://www.plannedparenthood.org].

[13] Unlike the Yuzpe method, progestin-only oral contraceptive preparations do not lend themselves to use as emergency contraception because of the large number of pills that need to be taken. For example, the "off-label" equivalent treatment is 40 tablets of a progestinonly oral contraceptive (Ovrette) taken within 120 hours after unprotected sex. NOT-2- LATE.com, The Emergency Contraception Website [http://ec.princeton.edu/worldwide/default.asp].

[14] A study conducted by WHO found that taking two 0.75 mg levonorgestrel pills together (one dose of 1.5 mg) was just as effective. Helena von Hertzen et al., "Low Dose Mifepristone and Two Regimens of Levonorgestrel for Emergency Contraception: a WHO Multicentre Randomised Trial," *Lancet*, v. 360, December 7, 2002, pp. 1803-1810.

[15] Horacio B. Croxatto et al., "Mechanisms of Action of Emergency Contraception," *Steroids*, v. 68, 2003, pp. 1095-1098.

[16] Ibid.

[17] E. Kesseru et al., "The Hormonal and Peripheral Effects of dl-Norgestrel in Postcoital Contraception," *Contraception*, v. 10, 1974, pp. 411-424.

[18] Horacio B. Croxatto et al., "Mechanisms of Action of Emergency Contraception," *Steroids*, v. 68, 2003, pp. 1095-1098.

[19] Ibid.

[20] Ibid.

[21] CRS Report RL30866, *Abortion: Termination of Early Pregnancy with RU-486(Mifepristone)*, by Judith A. Johnson.

[22] Anna Glasier, "Emergency Postcoital Contraception," *The New England Journal of Medicine*, v. 337, October 9, 1997, pp. 1058-1064.

[23] Comments by Dr. Daniel Davis, Medical Officer, FDA Division of Reproductive and Urologic Drugs, FDA Advisory Committee Meeting on Plan B, December 16, 2003 [http://www.fda.gov/ohrms/dockets/ac/03/transcripts/4015T1.htm].

[24] Cynthia C. Harper et al., "Tolerability of Levonorgestrel Emergency Contraception in Adolescents," American Journal of Obstetrics and Gynecology, v. 191, 2004, pp. 1158-1163; Tina R. Raine et al., "Direct Access to Emergency Contraception Through Pharmacies and Effect on Unintended Pregnancy and STIs," Journal of the American Medical Association, v. 293, January 5, 2005, pp. 54-62; and, Cynthia Harper et al., "The Effect of Increased Access to Emergency Contraception Among Young Adolescents," Obstetrics and Gynecology, v. 106, September 2005, pp. 483-491.

[25] WCC submitted a supplemental new drug application under section 505(b) of the Federal Food, Drug, and Cosmetic Act for Plan B. In February 2004, WCC sold the rights to market Plan B to Barr Pharmaceuticals. Barr had begun acting as the agent for WCC regarding Plan B in October 2003. [GAO Report, November 2005.] Duramed Research, Inc., the current sponsor of Plan B, is a subsidiary of Barr.

[26] See 21 C.F.R. 310.200(b) (2005).

[27] A transcript of the December 16, 2003, meeting can be found at [http://www.fda.gov/ohrms/dockets/ac/03/transcripts/4015T1.htm]

[28] The FDA advisory committee members voted on six questions; actual vote count is in brackets. **Question 1**: Does the actual use study demonstrate that consumers used the product as recommended in the proposed labeling? [27 yes, one no] **Question 2**: Are the actual use study data generalizable to the overall population of potential non-Rx users of Plan B? [27 yes, one no] **Question 3**: Based on the actual use study and literature review, is there evidence that non-Rx availability of Plan B leads to substitution of emergency contraceptive for the regular use of other methods of contraception? [zero yes, 28 no] **Question 4**: Do the data demonstrate that Plan B is safe for use in the nonprescription setting? [28 yes, zero no]

Question 5: Are the plans for introduction of Plan B into the non-Rx setting adequate with respect to consumer access and safe use? [22 yes, five no, one abstain] **Question 6**: Should Plan B be switched from prescription to non-prescription status? [27 votes: 23 yes, four no]

[29] Melanie A. Gold et al., "The Effects of Advance Provision of Emergency Contraception on Adolescent Women's Sexual and Contraceptive Behaviors," *Journal of Pediatric and Adolescent Gynecology*, v. 17, April 2004, pp. 87-96; and, Cynthia Harper et al., "The Effect of Increased Access to Emergency Contraception Among Young Adolescents," *Obstetrics and Gynecology*, v. 106, September 2005, pp. 483-491.

[30] U.S. Congress, Senate Committee on Health, Education, Labor and Pensions, Nomination of Lester M. Crawford, Hearing, 109th Congress, 1st sess., March 17, 2005, p. 16.

[31] ICF International, Comment Summary of FDA's Advanced Notice of a Proposed Rulemaking on September 1, 2005, Drug Approvals: Circumstances under which an Active Ingredient May Be Simultaneously Marketed in Both a Prescription Drug Product and an Over-the-counter Drug Product, May 19, 2006. Document found at [http://www.fda.gov/oc/planb/summary051906.html].

[32] Petition found at [http://clinton.senate.gov/news/statements/details.cfm?id=248085] and [http://murray.senate.gov/news.cfm?id=248094].

[33] Memorandum, Andrew von Eschenbach, FDA Acting Commissioner, August 23, 2006 [http://www.fda.gov/cder/drug/infopage/planB/avememo.pdf].

[34] This section was written by Vanessa K. Burrows, American Law Division, CRS.

[35] No. 05-366 (E.D.N.Y. filed January 21, 2005). Lester M. Crawford, former Acting Commissioner of the FDA, was the original named defendant.

[36] The State of Wisconsin filed a motion on March 20, 2006 seeking to be named as an additional plaintiff. The state cited its interests in pregnant teenagers and adolescent mothers, in current and potential Medicaid beneficiaries, in ensuring all children born in the state are wanted children, and in reducing the number of abortions and unwanted births. Wisconsin's motion to intervene was denied.

[37] No. 05-366, pp. 13, 34, 42 (fifth amended complaint filed October 10, 2006). The FDA did not approve Plan B for sale in locations such as supermarkets, gas stations, or convenience stores. *Id.* at 34. Plan B can only be distributed "through licensed drug wholesalers, retail operations with pharmacy services, and clinics with licensed healthcare practitioners." Press Release, FDA, FDA Approves Over-the-Counter Access for Plan B for Women 18 and Older, Prescription Remains Required for Those 17 and Under (August 24, 2006), available at [http://www.fda.gov/bbs/topics/NEWS/2006/NEW01436.html].

[38] No. 05-366, pp. 35-39 (fifth amended complaint filed October 10, 2006).

[39] *Id.* at 38, 41.

[40] *Id.* at 6, 41-42.

[41] *Id.* at 2; 5 U.S.C. § 706(1) - (2)(a), (c).

[42] No. 05-366, pp. 35-36 (fifth amended complaint filed October 10, 2006).

[43] *Id.* at 40.

[44] *Id.* at 31-33.

[45] Gardiner Harris, "FDA Approves Broader Access to Next-Day Pill," *New York Times*, August 25, 2006, p. A1.

[46] No. 05-366, pp. 13, 40 (fifth amended complaint filed October 10, 2006).

[47] No. 05-366, p. 33 (answer to fifth amended complaint filed March 5, 2007). The defendant did not have to file an answer to the plaintiffs' fourth amended complaint because the FDA approved Plan B for individuals 18 and older before the deadline for the defendant's answer.

[48] *Id.* at p. 11. The FDA allows citizens to petition for a switch of a drug from prescription to OTC status. 21 C.F.R. 310.200(b).

[49] *See* No. 05-366, p. 29 (answer to fifth amended complaint filed March 5, 2007) (referencing a letter from former FDA Commissioner Lester Crawford).

50 *Id.* at 24. The FDA also noted that the data required for OTC approval depends on the product. *Id.* at 30.

51 *Id.* at 2, 28. The question as to whether the FDA has created a third class of behind-thecounter drugs — in addition to prescription drugs and OTC drugs — is controversial. *See infra* text accompanying notes 63 to 67; Inside Washington Publishers, *FDA Policy Chief Reignites Debate over Third Drug Class*, FDA Week, May 18, 2007.

52 No. 05-366, p. 11-12 (answer to third amended complaint filed February 14, 2006). As a preliminary matter, the plaintiffs filed and a magistrate judge granted their motion seeking discovery of documents withheld under the deliberative process privilege. The judge also denied the FDA's request for a protective order quashing discovery or alternatively "an order prohibiting discovery from the White House," as he had done in February 2006 with a previous FDA request for a protective order preventing discovery. No. 05-366, pp. 1, 5 (Decision and Order, November 11, 2006). The FDA appealed the magistrate's decision on December 1, 2006.

53 No. 05-366, p. 14, 16 (answer to fifth amended complaint filed March 5, 2007).

54 *Id.* at 18.

55 No. 07-0561 (D.D.C. filed March 21, 2007) (plaintiff's amended complaint).

56 5 U.S.C. § 552(a)(6)(A)(i).

57 No. 07-0561, p. 1, 8 (D.D.C. filed July 16, 2007) (memorandum of law in support of defendant's motion to dismiss or, in the alternative, for summary judgment).

58 *Id.* at 9.

59 *Id.* at 2, 11-12.

60 No. 07-668 (D.D.C. filed April 12, 2007).

61 No. 07-668, p. 25 (D.D.C. filed April 12, 2007) (plaintiffs' complaint for declaratory and injunctive relief).

62 *Id.* at 2, 26-28.

63 *Id.* at 28.

64 *Id.* at 2-3, 29.

65 *Id.* at 29-30.

66 *Id.* at 2, 30-31.

67 No. 07-668, p. 10, 25, 31, 38, 41 (defendant's motion to dismiss filed June 29, 2007).

68 Except for the Medicaid coverage discussion at the end of this section, the information contained in this section was largely found in the following publication: Guttmacher Institute, "States Policies in Brief — Emergency Contraception," July 1, 2007 [http://www.guttmacher.org/statecenter/spibs/spib_EC.pdf].

69 Although FDA has the authority to determine the status for medications (OTC or prescription), states have the authority to determine who may prescribe prescription medications. Pharmacy access laws reflect the current prescription status for Plan B, as determined by the FDA [http://www.pharmacyaccess.org/pdfs/PharmacistFAQsOTC.pdf].

70 According to Steven Galson, Director of the FDA Center for Drug Evaluation and Research, the Plan B OTC decision will not effect these state regulations that allow the drug to be dispensed without prescription to people of all ages. Rita Rubin, "FDA Approves Over-The-Counter Sales of Plan B," *USA Today*, August 25, 2006, p. A2.

71 In addition, a few pharmacists in Montana provide Plan B under collaborative agreement with physicians. NOT-2-LATE.com, the Emergency Contraception Website [http://ec.princeton.edu/questions/what-fda-says.html].

72 Hilary Waldman, "Rell Signs Plan B Law; Changes Still Possible," *The Hartford Courant*, May 17, 2007.

73 For further information, see CRS Report RS22293, *Federal and State Laws Regarding Pharmacists Who Refuse to Distribute Contraceptives*, by Jody Feder.

74 *See* Wash. Admin. Code 246-869-010, 246-863-095; News Release, Washington State Department of Health, *Pharmacy Dispensing Rules go into Effect July 26* (July 17, 2007) [http://www.doh.wa.gov/Publicat/2007_news/07-116.htm].

[75] Wash. Admin. Code 246-869-010.

[76] Stormans, Inc. v. Seleck, No. 07-5374, p. 10, 12 (W.D.Wash. filed July 25, 2007). The plaintiffs allege violations of the equal protection and supremacy clauses of the U.S. Constitution, as well as violations of their rights to free exercise of religion and procedural due process. *Id.* at 15-17.

[77] Reuters, Wal-Mart Pharmacies to Carry Morning-After Pill, March 3, 2001.

[78] Michael Barbaro, "In Reversal, Wal-Mart Will Sell Contraceptives," *New York Times*, March 4, 2006.

[79] Information in this paragraph was found in the following publication: National Health Law Program, "Over the Counter or Out of Reach? A Report on Evolving State Medicaid Policies for Covering Emergency Contraception," June 2007, [http://www.healthlaw.org/].

[80] Ibid., p. 5-6.

[81] National Institute for Reproductive Health, "Expanding Medicaid Coverage for EC on the State Level," [http://www.prochoiceny.org/assets/files/ecreport.pdf].

[82] National Health Law Program, "Over the Counter or Out of Reach? A Report on Evolving State Medicaid Policies for Covering Emergency Contraception," June 2007, [http://www.healthlaw.org/]. Additional information on Medicaid coverage of emergency contraception can be found in the following document, Institute for Reproductive Health Access, National Health Law Program, National Latina Institute for Reproductive Health, and Ibis Reproductive Health, "Emergency Contraception & Medicaid: A State-by-State Analysis and Advocate's Toolkit," November 2005 [http://www.ibisreproductivehealth.org/pub/downloads/ECMedicaidAnalysisToolkit.pdf].

[83] Patricia Tjaden and Nancy Thoennes, "Extent, Nature, and Consequences of Rape Victimization: Findings From the National Violence Against Women Survey," U.S. Department of Justice, National Institute of Justice, January 2006 [http://www.ncjrs.gov/pdffiles1/nij/210346.pdf]. The National Crime Victimization Survey estimates that there were 209,880 rapes or sexual assaults in 2004 and 191,670 in 2005. Shannan M. Catalano, "Criminal Victimization, 2005," U.S. Department of Justice, Bureau of Justice Statistics, September 2006 [http://www.ojp.usdoj.gov/bjs/pub/pdf/cv05.pdf]. The Uniform Crime Reporting Program, of the U.S. Department of Justice, Federal Bureau of Investigation, states in the annual report "Crime in the United States" that there were an estimated 93,934 forcible rapes reported to law enforcement in 2005, a 1.2 percent decrease compared with 2004 [http://www.fbi.gov/ucr/05cius/offenses/violent_crime/forcible_rape.html]. ictim surveys indicate a larger number of rapes per year because less than 50 percent of rapes are reported to the police.

[84] Felicia H. Stewart and James Trussell, "Prevention of Pregnancy Resulting from Rape: A Neglected Preventive Health Measure," *American Journal of Preventive Health Medicine*, v. 19, November 2000, pp. 228-229.

[85] The DOJ guidelines are available at [http://www.ncjrs.org/pdffiles1/ovw/206554.pdf].

[86] Marie McCullough, Guidelines for Treating Rape Victims Omit Emergency Contraception, *The Philadelphia Inquirer*, December 31, 2004, p. A1.

[87] ACOG Educational Bulletin, Sexual Assault, *International Journal of Gynecology and Obstetrics*, v. 60, 1998, pp. 297-304; American College of Obstetricians and Gynecologists, Violence Against Women: Acute Care of Sexual Assault Victims (2004), available at [http://www.acog.org/departments/dept_notice.cfm?recno=17&bulletin=1625]; and American Public Health Association, 2003 Policy Statements, "2003-16 Providing Access to Emergency Contraception for Survivors of Sexual Assault," available at [http://www.gotoec.org/pdfs/Endorsement_APHA_SexualAssault.pdf].

[88] Center for Policy Alternatives, "Emergency Contraception for Sexual Assault Victims," found at [http://www.stateaction.org/issues/issue.cfm/issue/EC-SexualAssault.xml]; and Melanie A. Gold et al., Society for Adolescent Medicine, "Provision of Emergency Contraception to Adolescents," *Journal of Adolescent Health*, v. 35, July 2004 pp. 66-70.

[89] The letter is available online at [http://www.aclu.org/reproductiverights/gen/12743res

20050106.html].

90 The letter is available at [http://www.maloney.house.gov/documents/olddocs/choice/ 011305DOJ.pdf].

91 The White House, Office of the Press Secretary, Press Conference by the President, August 21, 2006 [http://www.whitehouse.gov/news/releases/2006/08/20060821.html].

92 Diedtra Henderson, "FDA Approves Sale of Morning-After Pill," *Boston Globe*, August 25, 2006.

93 Joyce Howard Price, "Plan B Allowed Over The Counter," *The Washington Times*, August 25, 2006.

94 C.B. Polis et al., "Advance Provision of Emergency Contraception for Pregnancy Prevention," Cochrane Database of Systematic Reviews, April 18, 2007, at [http://www.cochrane.org/reviews/en/ab005497.html].

95 Tina R. Raine et al., "Direct Access to Emergency Contraception Through Pharmacies and Effect on Unintended Pregnancy and STIs," *Journal of the American Medical Association*, v. 293, January 5, 2005, pp. 54-62.

96 Cynthia Harper et al., "The Effect of Increased Access to Emergency Contraception Among Young Adolescents," *Obstetrics and Gynecology*, v. 106, September 2005, pp. 483-491.

97 Ibid.

98 Melanie A. Gold et al., Society for Adolescent Medicine, "Provision of Emergency Contraception to Adolescents," *Journal of Adolescent Health*, v. 35, July 2004 pp. 66-70.

99 News Release, Statement of The American College of Obstetricians and Gynecologists, On the FDA's Approval of OTC Status for Plan B, August 24, 2006. Available at [http://www.acog.org/from_home/publications/press_releases/nr08-24-06.cfm].

100 Cynthia C. Harper et al., "Tolerability of Levonorgestrel Emergency Contraception in Adolescents," American Journal of Obstetrics and Gynecology, v. 191, 2004, pp. 1158-1163; Raine, "Direct Access to Emergency Contraception Through Pharmacies and Effect on Unintended Pregnancy and STIs," *Journal of the American Medical Association*, v. 293, January 5, 2005, pp. 54-62; Harper, "The Effect of Increased Access to Emergency Contraception Among Young Adolescents," *Obstetrics and Gynecology*, v. 106, September 2005, pp. 483-491.

101 Comment made by Dr. Julie A. Johnson, University of Florida Colleges of Pharmacy and Medicine, at the December 16, 2003 FDA Advisory Committee Meeting, page 225 of a 248-page transcript found at [http://www.fda.gov/ohrms/dockets/ac/ 03/transcripts/4015T1.htm].

102 Press Release, Human Life International, "President Bush Files for Divorse with Catholic Base," August 21, 2006 [http://www.hli.org/press_releases_divorcing_catholic_base.html].

103 David A. Grimes, "Emergency Contraception — Expanding Opportunities for Primary Prevention," *The New England Journal Of Medicine*, v. 337, October 9, 1997, pp. 1078-1079.

104 Barbara Martinez and Anna Wilde Mathews, "Easier Access to Contraceptives May Boost Costs," *The Wall Street Journal*, August 25, 2006, p. A8.

105 Ibid.

106 James Trussell et al., "Emergency Contraceptive Pills: A Simple Proposal to Reduce Unintended Pregnencies," *Family Planning Perspectives*, v. 24, November-December 1992, pp. 269-273.

107 Elizabeth G. Raymond, et al., "Population Effect of Increased Access to Emergency Contraceptive Pills — A Systematic Review," *Obstetrics and Gynecology*, v. 109, January 2007, pp. 181-188.

108 C.B. Polis et al., "Advance Provision of Emergency Contraception for Pregnancy Prevention," Cochrane Database of Systematic Reviews, April 18, 2007, at [http://www.cochrane.org/reviews/en/ab005497.html].

109 Ibid.

[110] Centers for Disease Control and Prevention, "National and State-Specific Pregnancy Rates Among States, 1995-1997," *MMWR Morbidity and Mortality Weekly Report*, v. 49, 2000, pp. 605-611.

[111] National Campaign to Prevent Teen Pregnancy, Not Just Another Single Issue: Teen Pregnancy Prevention's Link to Other Critical Social Issues, February 2002. Available at [http://www.teenpregnancy.org/resources/data/pdf/notjust.pdf].

[112] Barbara Martinez and Anna Wilde Mathews, "Easier Access to Contraceptives May Boost Costs, *The Wall Street Journal*, August 25, 2006, p. A8.

[113] Ibid.

[114] Jill Daly, "OTC Plan B Marks First Month," *Pittsburgh Post-Gazette*, December 13, 2006, p. F1.

[115] Rob Stein, "Plan B Use Surges, And So Does Controversy," *The Washington Post*, July 13, 2007, p. A1.

In: Abortion: Legislative and Legal Issues   ISBN: 978-1-60741-522-0
Editor: Kevin G. Nolan   © 2010 Nova Science Publishers, Inc.

Chapter 5

THE HISTORY AND EFFECT OF ABORTION CONSCIENCE CLAUSE LAWS*

Jon O. Shimabukuro

SUMMARY

Conscience clause laws allow medical providers to refuse to provide services to which they have religious or moral objections. In some cases, these laws are designed to excuse such providers from performing abortions. While substantive conscience clause legislation has not been approved, appropriations bills that include conscience clause provisions have been passed. This chapter describes the history of conscience clauses as they relate to abortion law and provides a legal analysis of the effects of such laws. The report also reviews recent proposed regulations to implement some of the conscience clause laws.

Conscience clause laws allow medical providers to refuse to provide services to which they have religious or moral objections. These laws are generally designed to reconcile "the conflict between religious health care providers who provide care in accordance with their religious beliefs and the patients who want access to medical care that these religious providers find objectionable."[1] Although conscience clause laws have grown to encompass protections for entities that object to a wide array of medical services and

---

* This is an edited, reformatted and augmented version of a CRS Report for Congress publication, Report RL34703, dated October 8, 2008.

procedures, such as providing contraceptives or terminating life-support, the original focus of conscience clause laws was on permitting health care providers to refuse to participate in abortion or sterilization procedures on religious or moral grounds.

HISTORICAL BACKGROUND

In 1973, Congress passed the first conscience clause law, commonly referred to as the Church Amendment,[2] in response to the U.S. Supreme Court's decision in *Roe v. Wade* and a U.S. district court decision that enjoined a Catholic hospital from prohibiting a physician from performing a sterilization procedure at the facility.[3] During consideration of the Church Amendment, Senator Frank Church explained the need for the conscience clause, stating, "It clears up any ambiguity in the present law by making it explicitly clear that it is not the intention of Congress to mandate religious hospitals to perform operations that are contrary to deeply held religious beliefs."[4]

The Church Amendment provides that individuals or entities that receive grants, contracts, loans, or loan guarantees under the Public Health Service Act (PHSA), the Community Mental Health Centers Act, or the Developmental Disabilities Services and Facilities Construction Act may not be required to perform abortions or sterilization procedures or make facilities or personnel available for the performance of such procedures if such performance "would be contrary to [the individual or entity's] religious beliefs or moral convictions."[5] The Church Amendment also prohibits entities that receive federal funds under the specified statutes or under a biomedical or behavioral research program administered by the Department of Health and Human Services (HHS) from engaging in employment discrimination against doctors or other medical personnel who either perform abortions or sterilization procedures or who refuse to perform such services on moral or religious grounds.[6]

By 1978, five years after the Court's decision in *Roe*, virtually all of the states had enacted conscience clause legislation in one form or another.[7] From 1978 to 1996, there was a lull in conscience clause activity, with one exception. When Congress enacted the Civil Rights Restoration Act in 1988, it adopted the Danforth Amendment, which mandates neutrality with respect to abortion.[8] Specifically, the amendment clarifies that Title IX of the Education Amendments of 1972, which prohibits sex discrimination in federally funded education programs, may not be construed to prohibit or require any individual or entity to provide or pay for abortion-related services, nor may it be construed to permit the imposition of a penalty on any person who has sought or received abortion-related services.[9]

Nearly a decade after the Danforth Amendment, Congress passed additional conscience provisions in the Omnibus Consolidated Rescissions and Appropriations Act of 1996.[10] Under the act, which added Section 245 to the PHSA, the federal government and state and local governments are prohibited from discriminating against health care entities that refuse to undergo abortion training, provide such training, perform abortions, or provide referrals for the relevant training or for abortions.[11] Section 245 protects doctors, medical students, and health training programs from being denied federal financial assistance or a license or certification that they would otherwise receive but for their refusal to provide abortion services or training.[12]

One year after passing the 1996 omnibus legislation, Congress again revisited the abortion conscience clause issue when it approved the Balanced Budget Act of 1997.[13] Concerned that managed care plans might seek to prevent doctors from informing patients about medical services not covered by their health plans, Congress amended the federal Medicare and Medicaid programs to prohibit managed care plans from restricting the ability of health care professionals to discuss the full range of treatment options with their patients.[14] The legislation, however, simultaneously exempted managed care providers under these programs from the requirement to provide, reimburse for, or provide coverage of a counseling or referral service if the managed care plan objects to the service on moral or religious grounds. Thus, a Medicare and Medicaid managed care plan cannot prevent providers from providing abortion counseling or referral services, but it can refuse to pay providers for providing such information, although the plan must notify new and existing enrollees of such a policy if it does indeed have one.[15]

The effect of the 1997 legislation was to extend the coverage of conscience clause laws beyond the individuals who provide medical care to the companies that pay for such care under the Medicare and Medicaid programs. The law allows Medicare and Medicaid-funded health plans to refuse to provide counseling and referral for abortion-related services. Earlier conscience clause laws permitted providers to opt out only of the actual provision of such services.[16]

The 1997 legislation would appear to have a broader impact than the 1973 Church Amendment, both in terms of its effect on the entities that may refuse to provide abortion services and on the individuals who wish to access such services. In a similar vein, recent abortion bills introduced in Congress have proposed changes that would expand the scope of current conscience clause laws. This legislation is discussed in the next section.

RECENT LEGISLATION AND ITS EFFECT ON EXISTING LAW

The Abortion Non-Discrimination Act (ANDA) has been introduced in every Congress since the 107th Congress.[17] In general, ANDA would amend the nondiscrimination provision in the PHSA to expand the definition of the term "health care entity" to include hospitals, provider-sponsored organizations, health maintenance organizations (HMOs), health insurance plans, or any other kind of health care facility, organization, or plan.

Supporters of ANDA maintain that expanding the definition of "health care entity" is necessary because some state legislatures and courts have weakened existing conscience clause protections, which proponents view as critical to shielding religious hospitals and other medical providers that oppose abortion. Opponents contend, however, that ANDA would impose serious restrictions on a woman's access to abortion. Critics also argue that ANDA would allow providers to drop abortion coverage not only for moral or religious reasons, but also for financial reasons, such as the desire to save money by reducing coverage.[18]

Although ANDA has not been considered by recent Congresses, conscience clause provisions with similar language were inserted in the FY2005, FY2006, and FY2008 appropriations measures for the Departments of Labor, HHS, and Education.[19] These provisions are commonly referred to as the Weldon Amendment because they were added to the FY2005 appropriations measure following the adoption of an amendment offered by Representative Dave Weldon. The language used in the appropriations measures has remained the same since 2004. The provisions state:

> None of the funds made available in this act may be made available to a Federal agency or program, or to a State or local government, if such agency, program, or government subjects any institutional or individual health care entity to discrimination on the basis that the health care entity does not provide, pay for, provide coverage of, or refer for abortions.[20]

The Weldon Amendment defines the term "health care entity" to include "an individual physician or other health care professional, a hospital, a provider-sponsored organization, a health maintenance organization, a health insurance plan, or any other kind of health care facility, organization, or plan."[21]

The Weldon Amendment prevents the federal government and state and local governments from enacting policies that require health care entities to provide or pay for certain abortion-related services. In addition, the Weldon Amendment increases both the number and type of health care providers and professionals who could refuse to provide abortion training or services without reprisals. For example, prior law protected only individual doctors or medical training programs that did not provide abortions or abortion training, and appeared to apply primarily in the medical education setting or to doctors in their individual practices. In contrast, the appropriations provisions allow large health insurance companies and HMOs to refuse to provide coverage or pay for abortions. Because an HMO's refusal to provide abortion-related services would affect a much larger number of patients than an individual doctor's refusal to provide such services, the Weldon Amendment has the potential of denying abortion-related services to a significantly expanded number of individuals.

Although the Weldon Amendment language is similar to the proposed ANDA, it differs in two important respects. First, ANDA would deny all federal funds to entities that engage in abortion-related discrimination. The Weldon Amendment, however, denies only those funds available under the annual Labor, HHS, and Education appropriations measure. Second, the passage of ANDA would result in permanent legislation, while the Weldon Amendment language remains in effect for only the relevant fiscal years. Thus, although the Weldon Amendment expands prior law, it provides for smaller penalties and is temporary in nature.

PROPOSED CONSCIENCE REGULATIONS

On August 26, 2008, HHS published a proposed rule to implement the Church Amendment, Section 245 of the PHSA, and the Weldon Amendment. HHS indicates that new regulations are needed because the "public and many health care providers are largely uninformed of the protections afforded to individuals and institutions" under the federal conscience clause laws.[22] In addition, the agency maintains that the development of a health care environment that is intolerant of certain religious beliefs and cultural traditions "may discourage individuals from diverse backgrounds from entering health care professions."[23]

The proposed regulations identify requirements and prohibitions for recipients of HHS funds. While these provisions are in many ways a reiteration of the statutory requirements and prohibitions, some argue that they would expand the reach of the conscience clause laws and possibly jeopardize the health of individuals by making it more difficult to obtain health care services and information.[24] These concerns would appear to be highlighted by some of the new definitions proposed by HHS for relevant terms. For example, the definitions for the terms "Health Service/Health Service Program" and "Assist in the Performance" seem to be broad enough to encompass a variety of activities. Such breadth could result in increased opportunities to refuse participation in the delivery of care or information.

The term "Health Service/Health Service Program" would be defined to include "any plan or program that provides health benefits, whether directly, through insurance, or otherwise, which is funded, in whole or in part, by [HHS]."[25] In the background section of the proposed rule, HHS indicates that it would construe the term broadly:

> Building on this broad definition, we propose that the term 'health service program' should be understood to include an activity related in any way to providing medicine, health care, or any other service related to health or wellness, including . . . health insurance programs where federal funds are used to provide access to health coverage (e.g., SCHIP, Medicaid, and Medicare Advantage). Similarly we propose that the term 'health service' means any service so provided.[26]

A broad understanding of the term could possibly lead to more individuals declining to provide health services or perform part of a health service program.

Under the proposed 45 C.F.R. § 88.4(d)(1), any entity that carries out any part of any health service program funded in whole or in part under a program administered by HHS could not require any individual to perform or assist in the performance of any part of the health service program if such service or activity would be contrary to his religious beliefs or moral convictions.[27] If the term "health service" is understood to include activities related in any way to providing medicine, it seems possible that the distribution of oral contraceptives could be affected.[28] Chain and independent pharmacies are, in fact, identified by HHS as entities that would be subject to the agency's proposed certification requirements.[29]

The term "Assist in the Performance" would be defined by the proposed regulations to mean "to participate in any activity with a reasonable connection to a procedure, health service or health service program, or research activity, so long as the individual involved is a part of the workforce of a Department-funded entity."[30] In the background section of the proposed rule, HHS indicates that it "proposes to interpret this term broadly, as encompassing individuals who are members of the workforce of the Department-funded entity performing the objectionable procedure."[31] Employees who clean the instruments used in a particular procedure, for example, would be considered by HHS to assist in the performance of that procedure.[32]

Opponents of the proposed regulations have criticized the possible breadth of the term "Assist in the Performance." Some have argued that the definition could provide conscience protections to seemingly tangential employees, such as staff members tasked with scheduling appointments, and others involved with purchasing and inventorying supplies.[33] While the use of the word "reasonable" in the definition for "Assist in the Performance" would seem to suggest a common sense approach to determining who would be covered within the definition, the agency's stated intention to interpret the term broadly could, in fact, provide such employees with conscience protections.

The comment period for the proposed rule ended on September 25, 2008. It appears that at least 2,074 comments were received by HHS prior to the end of the comment period.[34] The agency is expected to review the comments and make a decision about whether to issue a final rule.

End Notes

[1] Katherine A. White, *Crisis of Conscience: Reconciling Religious Health Care Providers' Beliefs and Patients' Rights*, 51 Stan. L. Rev. 1703, 1703 (1999).

[2] P.L. 93-45, § 401(b), (c), 87 Stat. 91 (1973). Additional conscience provisions supplemented the Church Amendment in 1974 and 1979. *See* P.L. 93-348, § 214(b), 88 Stat. 353 (1974); P.L. 96-76, § 208, 93 Stat. 583 (1979).

[3] *See* 119 Cong. Rec. 9,595 (1973) (statement of Sen. Church).

[4] *Id.* at 9,600.

[5] 42 U.S.C. § 300a-7(b).

[6] 42 U.S.C. § 300a-7(c).

[7] Rachel Benson Gold, Guttmacher Institute, Conscience Makes a Comeback in the Age of Managed Care (Feb. 1998), [http://www.guttmacher.org/pubs/tgr/01/1/gr010101.html].

[8] P.L. 100-259, § 3(b), 102 Stat. 28, 29 (1988).

[9] 20 U.S.C. § 1688.

[10] P.L. 104-134, 110 Stat. 1321 (1996).

[11] 42 U.S.C. § 238n(a)(1).

[12] 42 U.S.C. § 238n(b)(1).

[13] P.L. 105-33, 111 Stat. 251 (1997). The Medicare conscience clause provision is codified, as amended, at 42 U.S.C. § 1395w-22(j)(3)(B). The identical Medicaid conscience clause provision is codified, as amended, at 42 U.S.C. § 1396u-2(b)(3)(B).

[14] 42 U.S.C. § 1395w-22(j)(3)(A); 42 U.S.C. § 1396u-2(b)(3)(A).

[15] 42 U.S.C. § 1395w-22(j)(3)(B); 42 U.S.C. § 1396u-2(b)(3)(B).

[16] Despite the new exemptions regarding the provision of counseling and referral or abortion-related services, programs funded by Medicaid are nevertheless required to provide family planning services to their clients, either directly or through referral and payment to other providers. 42 U.S.C. § 1396d(a)(4)(C).

[17] S. 350, 110th Cong. (2007); S. 1983, 109th Cong (2005); H.R. 3664, 108th Cong. (2003); S. 1397, 108th Cong. (2003); H.R. 4691, 107th Cong (2002); S. 2008, 107th Cong. (2002).

[18] Reuters, *House Votes Hospitals May Avoid Abortions*, N.Y. Times, September 25, 2002, at A26.

[19] *See* P.L. 108-447, div. F, § 508(d), 118 Stat. 2809, 3163 (2004); P.L. 109-149, § 508(d), 119 Stat. 2833, 2879 (2005); H.R. 2764, 110th Cong., div. G, § 508(d) (2007). Appropriations for FY2007 were provided pursuant to H.J. Res 20, the Revised Continuing Appropriations Resolution, 2007, 110th Cong. (2007), and were subject to the same conditions that applied to FY2006 funds.

[20] P.L. 108-447, div. F, § 508(d)(1), 118 Stat. 2809, 3163 (2004); P.L. 109-149, § 508(d)(1), 119 Stat. 2833, 2879-80 (2005); H.R. 2764, 110th Cong., div. G, § 508(d)(1) (2007).

[21] P.L. 108-447, div. F, § 508(d)(2), 118 Stat. 2809, 3163 (2004); P.L. 109-149, § 508(d)(2), 119 Stat. 2833, 2880 (2005); H.R. 2764, 110th Cong., div. G, § 508(d)(2) (2007).

[22] Ensuring That Department of Health and Human Services Funds Do Not Support Coercive or Discriminatory Policies or Practices in Violation of Federal Law, 73 Fed. Reg. 50,274, 50,276 (Aug. 26, 2008) (to be codified at 45 C.F.R. pt. 88) (hereinafter referred to as "Conscience Regulations").

[23] *Id.*

[24] *See, e.g.*, Comments from Am. Civ. Liberties Union to U.S. Dept. of Health and Hum. Services 3 (Sept. 25, 2008), *available at* [http://www.aclu.org/images/asset_upload_file467_36942.pdf] ("[T]he expansion of the refusal statutes and the confusion caused by the Proposed Rule comes at the expense of the public's health, particularly the health of low-income women.").

[25] Conscience Regulations at 50,282.

[26] *Id.* at 50,278.

[27] *Id.* at 50,283.

[28] If a final rule is promulgated with few changes to the definition of the term "Health Service/Health Service Program," it may be necessary for a court to determine ultimately whether the definition encompasses the distribution of contraceptives. Although Michael O. Leavitt, the Secretary of HHS, has not discussed specifically the term "Health Service/Health Service Program," he has been reported as stating that some medical providers may want to "press the definition" and argue that some contraceptives are tantamount to abortion. See Stephanie Simon, *Rules Let Health Workers Deny Abortions — Regulation's Effect on Contraception Remains Unclear*, Wall St. J., Aug. 22, 2008, at A3.

[29] Conscience Regulations at 50,284. Under the proposed regulations, recipients and sub-recipients of HHS funds would be required to certify that they will not discriminate on the basis of past involvement in, or refusal to assist in the performance of an abortion or sterilization, and will not require involvement in procedures that violate an individual's conscience as part of any health service program in accord with all applicable sections of 45 C.F.R. part 88.

[30] *Id.* at 50,282.

[31] *Id.* at 50,277.

[32] *Id.*

[33] *See* Comments from Guttmacher Inst. to U.S. Dept. of Health and Hum. Services 4 (Sept. 24, 2008),   *available*   *at*   [http://www.guttmacher.org/media/resources/2008/09/24/ GuttmacherInstitute-re-ConscienceRegulation.pdf].

[34]   Information   on   the   comments   received   by   HHS   is   available   at [http://www.regulations.gov/fdmspublic/component/main?main=DocketDetail&d=HHSOS-2008-0011]. Additional concerns about the proposed regulations, including the possible conflict between the regulations and the provision of family planning services under Title X of the Public Health Service Act, have been expressed in the comments.

In: Abortion: Legislative and Legal Issues   ISBN: 978-1-60741-522-0
Editor: Kevin G. Nolan   © 2010 Nova Science Publishers, Inc.

Chapter 6

"PARTIAL-BIRTH" ABORTION AND THE 2006 TERM OF THE U.S. SUPREME COURT*

Jon O. Shimabukuro

SUMMARY

The Partial-Birth Abortion Ban Act ("PBABA" or "the act") was signed into law on November 5, 2003. Within two days of its enactment, the PBABA was enjoined by federal district courts in Nebraska, California, and New York. Since that time, the U.S. Courts of Appeals for the Second, Eighth, and Ninth Circuits have affirmed lower court decisions that have found the act unconstitutional.

This chapter examines *Gonzales v. Carhart* and *Gonzales v. Planned Parenthood*, the partial-birth abortion decisions from the Eighth and Ninth Circuits. In spring 2006, the U.S. Supreme Court agreed to review the two decisions. This chapter provides background information on the PBABA and explores the arguments put forth by the parties.

The Partial-Birth Abortion Ban Act ("PBABA" or "the act") was signed into law on November 5, 2003.[1] Within two days of its enactment, the PBABA was enjoined by federal district courts in Nebraska, California, and New York.[2] Since that time, the U.S. Courts of Appeals for the Second, Eighth, and

---

* This is an edited, reformatted and augmented version of a CRS Report for Congress publication, Report RL33778, dated January 4, 2007.

Ninth Circuits have affirmed lower court decisions that have found the act unconstitutional.[3]

In spring 2006, the U.S. Supreme Court agreed to review *Gonzales v. Carhart* and *Gonzales v. Planned Parenthood*, the partial-birth abortion decisions from the Eighth and Ninth Circuits. This chapter reviews the two cases and discusses the arguments put forth by the parties. The report also provides background information on the PBABA.

BACKGROUND

The PBABA was enacted after numerous attempts by Congress to limit the performance of an abortion procedure commonly referred to as "intact dilation and evacuation" or "dilation and extraction" ("D&X") by the medical community. Legislation to prohibit this procedure, described as "partial-birth abortion" by its opponents, was first passed by Congress in 1995 during the 104th Congress.[4] The PBABA of 1995 was vetoed by President Clinton because it did not include an exception that would allow the procedure to be used to protect the health of the mother. The President stated that "the bill does not allow women to protect themselves from serious threats to their health."[5] By refusing to allow the D&X procedure to be performed when a woman's health was in jeopardy, the President contended that "Congress has fashioned a bill that is consistent neither with the Constitution nor with sound public policy."[6]

During the 105th and 106th Congresses, Congress again passed legislation to prohibit the D&X procedure.[7] In 1997, during the 105th Congress, the President vetoed a partial-birth abortion measure on the grounds that it did not include a health exception.[8] In 2000, during the 106th Congress, the Senate did not appoint conferees to resolve differences between the House and Senate-passed versions of the legislation.

The partial-birth abortion measure that was enacted in 2003 prohibits a physician from knowingly performing a "partial-birth abortion" and killing a human fetus. The term "partial-birth abortion" is defined as an abortion in which the person performing the abortion "deliberately and intentionally" delivers a living fetus until a specified part of the fetus is outside the body of the mother for the purpose of performing an overt act that the person knows will kill the fetus, and performs the overt act that kills the fetus.[9]

Under the PBABA, a physician who knowingly performs a partial-birth abortion and kills a fetus will be subject to a fine, imprisonment for not more than two years, or both.[10] The act does not prohibit partial-birth abortions that are necessary to save the life of a mother whose life is endangered by a physical disorder, physical illness, or physical injury, including a life-endangering physical condition caused by or arising from the pregnancy itself. Thus, the PBABA allows an exception for partialbirth abortions to preserve the life of the mother. However, a similar exception to protect the health of the mother is not included in the act.

The PBABA provides a cause of action for certain individuals affected by the performance of a partial-birth abortion. The father of the fetus, if married to the mother at the time a partial-birth abortion is performed, and the maternal grandparents of the fetus, if the mother is under 18 years of age at the time of the abortion, may obtain appropriate relief, except when the pregnancy is the result of the plaintiff's criminal conduct or the plaintiff consented to the abortion.[11] For purposes of the prescribed cause of action, appropriate relief includes money damages for all psychological and physical injuries that arise as a result of the abortion.

The most notable difference between the PBABA and the other partial-birth abortion bills previously passed by Congress is the inclusion of a significant findings section in the law.[12] Section 2 of the act, which comprises more than half of the measure, identifies Congress's findings with respect to partial-birth abortion. For example, in this section, Congress "finds and declares" that a "moral, medical, and ethical consensus exists that the practice of performing a partial-birth abortion . . . is a gruesome and inhumane procedure that is never medically necessary and should be prohibited."[13] Concerns about the safety of the procedure, raised in testimony received during hearings in past Congresses, are also described in this section. Finally, the findings section includes a discussion of Supreme Court cases involving the Court's deference to congressional findings.

In his introduction of the PBABA, the act's sponsor, former Senator Rick Santorum, indicated that Congress may not only engage in factfinding, but that the Court will defer to such factfinding.[14] Senator Santorum indicated that Congress "is entitled to reach its own factual findings — findings that the Supreme Court accords great deference — and may enact legislation based on these findings."[15]

GONZALES V. CARHART AND GONZALES V. PLANNED PARENTHOOD

The decision to review both *Carhart* and *Planned Parenthood* provides the Court with the opportunity to evaluate all of the legal theories asserted against the constitutionality of the PBABA. In *Carhart*, the Eighth Circuit found the act unconstitutional solely on the grounds that it does not include an exception for abortions to protect the health of the mother. In *Planned Parenthood*, however, the Ninth Circuit concluded that the act is unconstitutional for three distinct reasons: it does not include an health exception; it imposes an undue burden on a woman's ability to have an abortion by prohibiting both the D&X procedure and the standard dilation and evacuation ("D&E") procedure;[16] and it is unconstitutionally vague, thus depriving fair notice to physicians about what is prohibited.[17] The Court's decision to review *Planned Parenthood*, made nearly four months after its decision to review *Carhart*, was hailed by some members of the pro-choice community who believe that the Ninth Circuit decision provides a more complete record on the likely impact of the statute.[18]

The government has made three arguments in support of the PBABA.[19] First, the government maintains that the absence of a health exception does not impose an undue burden on a woman's ability to have an abortion. Second, the government contends that the act is not unconstitutionally vague or overbroad. Finally, the government argues that even if the Court is able to identify some aspect of the act that is invalid, it may be possible to craft narrower injunctive relief consistent with *Ayotte v. Planned Parenthood of Northern New England*, the Court's 2006 decision in which it held that the First Circuit erred in striking down a state parental consent statute in its entirety.[20]

HEALTH EXCEPTION

In *Stenberg v. Carhart*, a 2000 case involving the constitutionality of a Nebraska partial-birth abortion statute, the Court invalidated the state law because it failed to include an exception to protect the health of the mother and because the language used to define the prohibited procedure was too vague.[21] The government asserts that a proper reading of *Stenberg* requires a statute that regulates abortion, but lacks an health exception, to be upheld unless it would create significant health risks and thereby impose an undue burden on a large fraction of women. The government maintains that congressional factfinding supports both the position that the absence of a health exception does not create significant health risks for a large fraction of women, and that partial-birth abortion is never medically indicated to preserve the health of a mother. According to the government, the testimony of physicians who appeared before Congress and other evidence in the legislative record emphasize that a ban on partial-birth abortion would not endanger a woman's health because the procedure is never medically necessary.

In addition, the government argues that congressional factfinding should be afforded a high degree of deference. Citing *Turner Broadcasting System, Inc. v. FCC*, two cases from 1994 and 1997, commonly referred to as *Turner I* and *Turner II*,[22] involving federal cable legislation and "must-carry" obligations imposed on cable operators, the government notes that the Court has "deferred to congressional factual findings in a wide variety of contexts and with regard to a wide variety of constitutional claims."[23] In *Turner I*, the Court indicated that reviewing courts must accord substantial deference to the predictive judgments of Congress when evaluating the constitutionality of a statute. The Court observed that a reviewing court's sole obligation is "to assure that, in formulating its judgments, Congress has drawn reasonable inferences based on substantial evidence."[24]

The respondents, Planned Parenthood and Carhart, challenge the government's reliance on Congress's findings and the belief that the Court owes great deference to such findings, and also argue that the government's use of a "significant health risks" standard is inappropriate.[25] Planned Parenthood maintains that the *Stenberg* Court was guided by *Planned Parenthood of Southeastern Pennsylvania v. Casey*, the Court's 2002 abortion decision, and the conclusion that a medical emergency exception should be broad enough to ensure that compliance with an abortion restriction would not in any way pose a significant threat to the life or health of a woman. Thus, in *Stenberg*, the Court held that to prevent a significant threat to the life or health of a woman, a "method-specific ban" must have a health exception if substantial medical authority supports the proposition that banning that method could endanger women's health.

Planned Parenthood contends that by requiring substantial medical authority "as the quantum of proof for whether a health exception is constitutionally required," individual physicians are prevented from acting with unfettered discretion and reasonable differences of medical opinion are tolerated.[26] In short, Planned Parenthood argues that the government's failure to address the "substantial medical authority" standard articulated in *Stenberg* is not "constitutionally tolerable."[27] By considering only whether significant health risks are imposed on a large fraction of women, some women could be forced to endure significant health risks in contravention of *Roe*'s essential holding, that the health of pregnant women must remain paramount when regulating abortion.

Planned Parenthood and Carhart dispute the government's position that a partial-birth abortion is never medically necessary. They assert that during consideration of the act, numerous physicians and medical groups expressed concerns about the legislation preventing them from using the safest procedures.[28] Examples of specific circumstances when D&X offered particular advantages were also identified. Some physicians stated that D&X involves less risk of uterine perforation or cervical laceration, and reduces the risk of retained fetal tissue. The respondents contend that a reduced risk of complications is particularly important for women with serious medical problems because such women do not have the "physiological reserves" to cope with the complications.[29] Additional support for the use of D&X under certain circumstances to preserve the health of the woman was also identified during the district court trials of the two cases.

In addition to challenging the factual findings defended by the government, the respondents question the government's position that such findings demand great deference from the Court. In particular, the respondents dispute the government's reliance on *Turner I* and *Turner II*.

Carhart contends that the *Turner* cases are inapplicable with regard to the PBABA. Carhart argues that the Court has never deferred to congressional findings in a case where Congress uses such findings in an attempt to alter the meaning and scope of substantive constitutional rights.[30] Carhart maintains that an extension of *Turner* to this case would "effectively provide Congress with carte blanche to violate the Constitution simply by making carefully chosen 'findings.'"[31] According to Carhart, deference is appropriate only when legislation involves areas where Congress has particular expertise and courts have previously shown deference to congressional findings.

Moreover, Carhart stresses that the *Turner* cases require deference only with regard to Congress's predictive judgments. Carhart argues that these judgments pertain to "circumstances in which Congress must make its best predictions concerning how an industry will evolve or how individuals will respond to economic motivations."[32] From this viewpoint, Congress's findings on the medical necessity of the partial-birth abortion procedure do not involve similar predictions.

Like Carhart, Planned Parenthood believes that the factual findings are not entitled to deference. Planned Parenthood argues that the findings are "simply a bald-faced attempt to end-run *Stenberg*'s constitutional rule."[33] In addition, Planned Parenthood emphasizes that the *Turner* cases require deference only when Congress has drawn reasonable inferences based on substantial evidence. In this case, Planned Parenthood believes that Congress's findings are unreasonable and therefore not entitled to deference. Planned Parenthood notes that all three district courts to have considered the validity of the PBABA have concluded that the findings are not reasonable and merit no deference. For example, the federal district court in *Planned Parenthood* found that "all of the government's own witnesses disagreed with many of the specific congressional findings."[34]

UNDUE BURDEN AND THE OVERBREADTH DOCTRINE

The Ninth Circuit's invalidation of the PBABA was based, in part, on the statute being unconstitutionally overbroad.[35] The overbreadth doctrine is concerned generally with a statute's precision and the possibility of restricting constitutionally protected activities. In *Stenberg*, the Court found that the Nebraska partial-birth abortion statute was improperly overbroad because it defined a "partial-birth abortion" in such a way as to prohibit the standard D&E procedure as well as the D&X procedure. As a result, the statute imposed an undue burden on a woman's access to an abortion. Similar arguments have been made against the PBABA.

The government maintains that the federal definition for a "partial-birth abortion" is different from the Nebraska definition and thus, should not imperil the statute. The government argues that the federal definition differs in two critical ways. First, by identifying "anatomical landmarks," a partial-birth abortion under the act could not encompass the D&E procedure.[36] Under the act, a partial-birth abortion involves the delivery of the fetus until either the entire fetal head or any part of the fetal trunk past the navel is outside the body of the mother. During a D&E procedure, the government asserts, only a small portion of the fetus, such as a foot or an arm, may be brought outside the body of the mother. Second, the government contends that the federal statute applies only where the person performing the abortion also completes an "overt act" that kills the fetus.[37] Thus, by requiring the overt act, the act does not apply to the D&E procedure, where the delivery of a portion of the fetus and the dismemberment of the fetus are indistinguishable.

The respondents maintain that the act's definition for a partial-birth abortion could still encompass abortions involving the D&E procedure. Findings by the district court in *Planned Parenthood* indicate that there is no standard degree to which a fetus is extracted during a D&E procedure before an obstructing part of the fetus may be disarticulated or reduced in size. Thus, the respondents argue that the extraction of the fetus to the point of the anatomic landmarks may occur during a standard D&E abortion.

The respondents also dispute the government's reliance on the completion of an overt act as sufficient to distinguish the partial-birth abortion procedure from the standard D&E procedure.[38] They maintain that during a D&E abortion, a physician may have to perform the overt act of disarticulation or the compressing or decompressing of a fetal part to complete the abortion. These acts are distinct from the extraction of the fetus and would seem to constitute an overt act. The respondents state that even the government has found disarticulation to be an overt act. Carhart notes that the overt act requirement "does not effectively exclude D&E procedures . . . because, as the Government concedes, the overt act may include disarticulation."[39] If such an act is necessary and the fetus has been extracted to the point of the anatomic landmarks, the physician will have arguably performed a partial-birth abortion.

VAGUENESS

The doctrine of vagueness involves the clarity of a statute. A statute must be drawn with sufficient clarity to inform people of the conduct that must be avoided to avert the statute's penalties. The Ninth Circuit concluded that the PBABA was void for vagueness because it failed to clearly define the medical procedures that are prohibited and thus deprived physicians fair notice of improper conduct and encouraged arbitrary enforcement.[40]

The government contends that the Constitution does not require "impossible standards of clarity."[41] Rather, a statute must simply give a person of ordinary intelligence a "reasonable opportunity" to know what is prohibited, so that he may act accordingly.[42] The government believes that the act "readily satisfies the relatively modest requirements of the void-for-vagueness doctrine."[43] The government maintains that the statute prohibits a particular type of abortion in which the physician "deliberately and intentionally" delivers a living fetus to a specific anatomical point outside the body of the mother for the purpose of knowingly performing an overt act that will kill the fetus. Moreover, the government asserts that the act contains no ambiguous terms or phrases.

The respondents maintain that the act is unconstitutionally vague because it not only fails to clearly define the prohibited procedure, but also forces physicians to "guess at [the act's] meaning and differ as to its application."[44] The respondents stress that some D&E abortions do satisfy the anatomical landmark requirements identified in the act, and thus would seem to constitute partial-birth abortions under the statute. Similarly, some acts undertaken as part of a D&E procedure may constitute an overt act for purposes of the statute, thus exposing a physician to liability. Arguing that physicians will have to guess at the meaning of the act's language and the government's "strained interpretations," the respondents maintain that the act is unconstitutionally vague.[45]

NARROWER INJUNCTIVE RELIEF

Although it maintains firmly that the PBABA is constitutional, the government suggests that it may be possible to craft more narrow injunctive relief, rather than complete invalidation, if some aspect of the act is found unconstitutional.[46] In *Ayotte*, the Court concluded that the First Circuit acted inappropriately when it invalidated a state parental consent statute in its entirety. Although the state law at issue did not include a health exception, the Court held that a more narrow remedy was appropriate because only some aspects of the law raised constitutional concerns. The Court returned the case to the court of appeals with instructions to craft a narrower remedy.

The respondents assert that the act should be enjoined in its entirety. Citing *Ayotte*, they discuss the three "interrelated principles" identified by Justice O'Connor in that case that inform the Court's approach to remedies.[47] First, the Court should not nullify more of a statute than is necessary. Second, the Court must be mindful that its constitutional mandate and institutional competence are limited. Finally, the Court cannot use its remedial powers to circumvent the intent of the legislature. With regard to this third principle, Justice O'Connor noted: "After finding an application or portion of a statute unconstitutional, we must next ask: Would the legislature have preferred what is left of its statute to no statute at all?"[48]

If the Court determines that the PBABA is unconstitutional because of its failure to include a health exception, the respondents contend that a remedy that somehow adds a health exception to the act would be inappropriate.[49]

They argue that because Congress expressly rejected even a narrow health exception when it passed the act, the Court would engage in the kind of "line-drawing" it rejected in *Ayotte* if it permitted such a remedy.

Similarly, if the Court determines that the act is unconstitutional because it is vague or overbroad, the respondents argue that it would be impermissible to "engraft" either a narrower definition for the term "partial-birth abortion" or a clearer distinction between partial-birth abortion and a standard D&E abortion.[50] Acknowledging the Court's disposition of the Nebraska statute in *Stenberg*, the respondents contend that the federal law should be similarly invalidated in toto. According to the respondents, because the act implicates many, if not all, D&E abortions, it unduly burdens a large fraction of affected women and must be facially invalidated. Planned Parenthood also contends that any attempt to establish a distinction between a partial-birth abortion and a D&E abortion would "merely propagate the substantive problems with the act that lead to the need for a remedy in the first place. In other words, it would be no cure at all."[51]

CONCLUSION

The Court's consideration of *Carhart* and *Planned Parenthood* has garnered widespread interest not just because of the possible invalidation of the PBABA. Justice O'Connor's retirement in early 2006 and the appointment of two new seemingly conservative Justices have prompted many to believe that the Court may use this opportunity to establish new standards with regard to the evaluation of all laws that regulate abortion. For example, the Court may explore whether a health exception is always needed in an abortion-related statute. The Court may also clarify whether the term "health" should continue to be broadly understood to include not only physical, but mental and emotional health.

Considerable attention has focused on Justice Kennedy because of Justice O'Connor's retirement, his dissent in *Stenberg*, and his position as a "swing vote" on the Court. While Justice Kennedy has been protective of the Court's role in defining the scope of constitutional rights, his support for the Nebraska partial-birth abortion statute has been noted.

During the oral arguments in *Carhart* and *Planned Parenthood* before the Court on November 6, 2006, Justice Kennedy's questions and comments suggested arguably that he may have some skepticism about the act.[52] Justices Scalia and Thomas, both part of the dissent in *Stenberg*, are widely expected to support the validity of the PBABA. If they were joined by the Court's newest justices, Chief Justice Roberts and Justice Alito, as well as Justice Kennedy, the act would be upheld.

End Notes

[1] P.L. 108-105, 117 Stat. 1201 (2003).

[2] For additional information on the Partial-Birth Abortion Ban Act litigation, see CRS Report RL30415, *Partial-Birth Abortion: Recent Developments in the Law*, by Jon O. Shimabukuro.

[3] *See* National Abortion Federation v. Gonzales, 437 F.3d 278 (2[d] Cir. 2006); Carhart v. Gonzales, 413 F.3d 791 (8th Cir. 2005); Planned Parenthood v. Gonzales, 435 F.3d 1163 (9th Cir. 2006).

[4] H.R. 1833, 104th Cong. (1995).

[5] Message to the House of Representatives Returning Without Approval Partial Birth Abortion Legislation, 32 Weekly Comp. Pres. Doc. 645 (Apr. 10, 1996).

[6] *Id.* For additional information on abortion generally, see CRS Report 95-724, *Abortion Law Development: A Brief Overview*, by Karen J. Lewis and Jon O. Shimabukuro. In *Roe v. Wade*, 410 U.S. 113 (1973), the U.S. Supreme Court determined that a restriction on abortion is unconstitutional if it does not recognize an exception for abortions that are necessary to preserve the life or health of the mother. The Court has reaffirmed that position in subsequent abortion decisions.

[7] H.R. 1122, 105th Cong. (1997); H.R. 3660, 106th Cong. (2000); S. 1692, 106th Cong. (2000).

[8] Message to the House of Representatives Returning Without Approval Partial Birth Abortion Legislation, 33 Weekly Comp. Pres. Doc. 41 (Oct. 13, 1997).

[9] P.L. 108-105, § 3, 117 Stat. 1201, 1206 (2003).

[10] *Id.*

[11] *Id.*

[12] *See* P.L. 108-105, § 2, 117 Stat. 1201 (2003)

[13] *Id.*

[14] 149 Cong. Rec. S2523 (daily ed. Feb. 14, 2003) (statement of Sen. Santorum).

[15] *Id.*

[16] The standard D&E procedure is the most common method of abortion in the second trimester. The standard D&E procedure is distinct from the intact D&E procedure, which is performed generally in the latter part of the second trimester. For additional discussion on D&E, *see* Shimabukuro, *supra* note 2.

[17] In *Planned Parenthood of Southeastern Pennsylvania v. Casey*, 505 U.S. 833 (1992), the U.S. Supreme Court concluded that a restriction on abortion that imposes an undue burden on woman's right to terminate a pregnancy would be found unconstitutional. The *Casey* Court defined an undue burden as "a substantial obstacle in the path of a woman seeking an abortion of a nonviable fetus." For additional information on *Casey*, *see* Lewis and Shimabukuro, *supra* note 6 at 14.

[18] *See* Linda Greenhouse, *Justices to Expand Review of "Partial-Birth" Abortion Ban*, N.Y. Times, June 20, 2006, at A14.

[19] Brief for the Petitioner, Gonzales v. Carhart (No. 05-380), 2006 WL 1436690; Brief for the Petitioner, Gonzales v. Planned Parenthood (No. 05-1382), 2006 WL 2282123.

[20] 126 S.Ct. 961 (2006).

[21] 530 U.S. 914 (2000).

[22] 512 U.S. 622 (1994) ("Turner I"); 520 U.S. 180 (1997) ("Turner II").

[23] Brief for the Petitioner at 21, *Carhart* (No. 05-380).

[24] *Turner I*, 512 U.S. at 666.

[25] Brief of Respondents, Gonzales v. Planned Parenthood (No. 05-1382), 2006 WL 2725691; Brief of Respondents, Gonzales v. Carhart (No. 05-380), 2006 WL 2345934.

[26] Brief of Respondents at 13, *Planned Parenthood* (No. 05-1382).

[27] *Id*. at 14.

[28] *Id*. at 5 ("In 2003, during the 108th Congress which enacted the act, highly-credentialed physicians and nationally recognized major medical groups, including [the American College of Obstetricians & Gynecologists], submitted statements to Congress opposing the act.").

[29] *See* Brief of Respondents at 22, *Planned Parenthood* (No. 05-1382).

[30] Brief of Respondents at 24, *Carhart* (No. 05-380).

[31] *Id*.

[32] *Id*. at 32.

[33] Brief of Respondents at 24, *Planned Parenthood* (No. 05-1382).

[34] *See Id*. at 27.

[35] *See Planned Parenthood*, 435 F.3d at 1179 ("Contrary to the government's claim, properly construed the act covers non-intact as well as intact D&Es. As a result, despite containing some provisions that are different in form from those in the Nebraska statute, the act is sufficiently broad to cause those who perform non-intact D&E procedures to 'fear prosecution, conviction, and imprisonment' (citation omitted). The resulting chilling effect on doctors' willingness to perform previability post-first trimester abortions would impose an undue burden on the constitutional rights of women.").

[36] Brief for the Petitioner at 31, *Planned Parenthood* (No. 05-1382).

[37] *Id*.

[38] *See* Brief of Respondents at 41, *Carhart* (No. 05-380).

[39] *Id*.

[40] *See Planned Parenthood*, 435 F.3d at 1181-82.

[41] *See* Brief for the Petitioner at 36, *Planned Parenthood* (No. 05-1382).

[42] *Id*.

[43] Brief for the Petitioner at 48, *Carhart* (No. 05-380).

[44] *See* Brief of Respondents at 44, *Planned Parenthood* (No. 05-1382).

[45] Brief of Respondents at 45, *Planned Parenthood* (No. 05-1382).

[46] Brief for the Petitioner at 49-50, *Carhart* (No. 05-380); Brief for the Petitioner at 40, *Planned Parenthood* (No. 05-1382).

[47] *See* Brief of Respondents at 47-48, *Carhart* (No. 05-380); Brief of Respondents at 48-49, *Planned Parenthood* (No. 05-1382).

[48] *Ayotte*, 126 S.Ct. at 968.

[49] Brief of Respondents at 48-49, *Carhart* (No. 05-380); Brief of Respondents at 47-48, *Planned Parenthood* (No. 05-1382).

[50] *See* Brief for Respondent at 49, *Planned Parenthood* (No. 05-1382).

[51] *Id*. at 50.

[52] *See* Transcript of Oral Argument, Gonzales v. Carhart, No. 05-380 (2006), *available at* [http://www.supremecourtus.gov/oral_arguments/argument_transcripts/05-380.pdf]; Transcript of Oral Argument, Gonzales v. Planned Parenthood, No. 05-1382 (2006), *available at* [http://www.supremecourtus.gov/oral_arguments/argument_transcripts/05-1382.pdf]. In an exchange with the Solicitor General, Justice Kennedy stated that the D&X procedure could be warranted in some situations. In response to the Solicitor General's assertion that prohibiting the D&X procedure would pose little risk to a woman's health because the standard D&E procedure "has been well-tested and works every single time as a way to terminate the pregnancy,"Justice Kennedy maintained: "[B]ut there is a risk if the uterine wall is compromised by cancer or some forms of preeclampsia and it's very thin, there's a risk of being punctured."

In: Abortion: Legislative and Legal Issues   ISBN: 978-1-60741-522-0
Editor: Kevin G. Nolan   © 2010 Nova Science Publishers, Inc.

Chapter 7

PARTIAL-BIRTH ABORTION: RECENT DEVELOPMENTS IN THE LAW*

Jon O. Shimabukuro

SUMMARY

The term "partial-birth abortion" refers generally to an abortion procedure where the fetus is removed intact from a woman's body. The procedure is described by the medical community as "intact dilation and evacuation" or "dilation and extraction" ("D & X") depending on the presentation of the fetus. Intact dilation and evacuation involves a vertex or "head first" presentation, the induced dilation of the cervix, the collapsing of the skull, and the extraction of the entire fetus through the cervix. D & X involves a breech or "feet first" presentation, the induced dilation of the cervix, the removal of the fetal body through the cervix, the collapsing of the skull, and the extraction of the fetus through the cervix.

Since 1995, at least thirty-one states have enacted laws banning partial-birth abortions. Although many of these laws have not taken effect because of temporary or permanent injunctions, they remain contentious to both pro-life advocates and those who support a woman's right to choose. This chapter discusses the U.S. Supreme Court's decision in *Stenberg v. Carhart*, a case involving the constitutionality of Nebraska's partial-birth abortion ban statute.

---

* This is an edited, reformatted and augmented version of a CRS Report for Congress publication, Report RL30415, dated January 14, 2008.

In *Stenberg*, the Court invalidated the Nebraska statute because it lacked an exception for the performance of the partial-birth abortion procedure when necessary to protect the health of the mother, and because it imposed an undue burden on a woman's ability to have an abortion.

This chapter also reviews various legislative attempts to restrict partial-birth abortions during the 106th, 107th, and 108th Congresses. S. 3, the Partial-Birth Abortion Ban Act of 2003, was signed by the President on November 4, 2003. On April 18, 2007, the Court upheld the act, finding that, as a facial matter, it is not unconstitutionally vague and does not impose an undue burden on a woman's right to terminate her pregnancy. In reaching its conclusion in *Gonzales v. Carhart*, the Court distinguished the federal statute from the Nebraska law at issue in *Stenberg*.

INTRODUCTION

Since 1995, at least thirty-one states have enacted laws banning the so-called "partial-birth" abortion procedure. Although many of these laws have not taken effect because of permanent injunctions, they remain contentious to both pro-life advocates and those who support a woman's right to choose.[1] The concern over partial-birth abortion has been shared by Congress. Congress passed bans on the partial-birth abortion procedure in both the 104th and 105th Congresses.[2] Unable to overcome presidential vetoes during both congressional terms, the Partial-Birth Abortion Ban Act was reintroduced in each successive Congress until its enactment in 2003. S. 3, the Partial-Birth Abortion Ban Act of 2003, was passed by Congress in October 2003. The measure was signed by the President on November 5, 2003.

The U.S. Supreme Court has also addressed the performance of partial-birth abortions. In *Stenberg v. Carhart*, a 2000 case, the Court invalidated a Nebraska statute that prohibited the performance of such abortions. Prior to this decision, the U.S. Courts of Appeals remained divided on the legitimacy of state statutes banning partial-birth abortions.[3] In *Gonzales v. Carhart*, a 2007 case, the Court upheld the Partial-Birth Abortion Ban Act of 2003, finding that, as a facial matter, it is not unconstitutionally vague and does not impose an undue burden on a woman's right to terminate her pregnancy.[4] This chapter discusses the Court's decisions and the partial-birth abortion measures in the 106th, 107th, and 108th Congresses.

BACKGROUND

The Supreme Court has held that a woman has a constitutional right to choose whether to terminate her pregnancy.[5] Although a state cannot prohibit a woman from having an abortion, it can promote its interest in potential human life by regulating, and even proscribing, abortion after fetal viability so long as it allows an exception for abortions that are necessary for the preservation of the life or health of the mother.[6] In *Planned Parenthood of Southeastern Pennsylvania v. Casey*, the Court expanded a state's authority to regulate abortion by permitting regulation at the previability stage so long as such regulation does not place an "undue burden" on a woman's ability to have an abortion.[7]

The term "partial-birth abortion" refers generally to an abortion procedure where the fetus is removed intact from a woman's body. The procedure is described by the medical community as "intact dilation and evacuation" or "dilation and extraction" ("D & X") depending on the presentation of the fetus.[8] Intact dilation and evacuation involves a vertex or "head first" presentation, the induced dilation of the cervix, the collapsing of the skull, and the extraction of the entire fetus through the cervix.[9] D & X involves a breech or "feet first" presentation, the induced dilation of the cervix, the removal of the fetal body through the cervix, the collapsing of the skull, and the extraction of the fetus through the cervix.[10] This chapter uses the term "D & X" to encompass both procedures.

D & X is one of several abortion methods. The principal methods of abortion are suction curettage, induction, and standard dilation and evacuation ("D & E").[11] The decision to perform one abortion method over another usually depends on the gestational age of the fetus. During the first trimester, the most common method of abortion is suction curettage.[12] Suction curettage involves the evacuation of the uterine cavity by suction. The embryo or fetus is separated from the placenta either by scraping or vacuum pressure before being removed by suction. Induction may be performed either early in the pregnancy or in the second trimester. In this procedure, the fetus is forced from the uterus by inducing preterm labor.

D & E is the most common method of abortion in the second trimester.[13] Suction curettage is no longer viable because the fetus is too large in the second trimester to remove by suction alone. D & E involves the dilation of the cervix and the dismemberment of the fetus inside the uterus. Fetal parts are later removed from the uterus either with forceps or by suction.

D & X is typically performed late in the second trimester between the twentieth and twenty-fourth weeks of pregnancy. Although the medical advantages of D & X have been asserted, the nature of the procedure has prompted pro-life advocates to characterize D & X as something akin to infanticide.[14]

In *Women's Medical Professional Corporation v. Voinovich*, the U.S. Court of Appeals for the Sixth Circuit discussed the differences between the D & E and D & X procedures in reference to an Ohio act that banned partial-birth abortions:

> The primary distinction between the two procedures is that the D & E procedure results in a dismembered fetus while the D & X procedure results in a relatively intact fetus. More specifically, the D & E procedure involves dismembering the fetus in utero before compressing the skull by means of suction, while the D & X procedure involves removing intact all but the head of the fetus from the uterus and then compressing the skull by means of suction. In both procedures, the fetal head must be compressed, because it is usually too large to pass through a woman's dilated cervix. In the D & E procedure, this is typically accomplished by either suctioning the intracranial matter or by crushing the skull, while in the D & X procedure it is always accomplished by suctioning the intracranial matter.[15]

The procedural similarities between the D & E and D & X procedures have contributed to the concern that the language of partial-birth abortion bans may prohibit both methods of abortion.

Plaintiffs challenging partial-birth abortion statutes have generally sought the invalidation of such statutes on the basis of two arguments: first, that the statutes are unconstitutionally vague, and second, that the statutes are unconstitutional because they impose an undue burden on a woman's ability to obtain an abortion. The Supreme Court has held that an enactment is void for vagueness if its prohibitions are not clearly defined.[16] Vague laws are found unconstitutional because they fail to give people of ordinary intelligence a reasonable opportunity to know what is prohibited and thus allow them to act lawfully.[17] Moreover, the inability to provide explicit standards is feared to result in the arbitrary and discriminatory enforcement of a statute.

The undue burden standard was adopted by the Court in *Casey*. In that case, the Court held that a state could enact abortion regulations at the pre-viability stage so long as an "undue burden" is not placed on a woman's ability to have an abortion. Any regulation which "has the purpose or effect of placing a substantial obstacle in the path of a woman seeking an abortion" creates an undue burden and is invalid.[18]

The Sixth Circuit was the first to consider whether a ban on partial-birth abortions imposes an undue burden on a woman's ability to have an abortion. In *Voinovich*, the court found that an Ohio statute that attempted to ban the D & X procedure was unconstitutional under *Casey*. The court determined that the language of the statute targeted the D & X procedure, but encompassed the D & E procedure. Because the D & E procedure is the most common method of second trimester abortions, the court contended that the statute created an undue burden on women seeking abortions at this point in their pregnancies.

STENBERG V. CARHART

In *Stenberg v. Carhart*, a Nebraska physician who performed abortions at a specialized abortion facility sought a declaration that Nebraska's partial-birth abortion ban statute violated the U.S. Constitution.[19] The Nebraska statute provided:

> No partial birth abortion shall be performed in this state, unless such procedure is necessary to save the life of the mother whose life is endangered by a physical disorder, physical illness, or physical injury, including a life-endangering physical condition caused by or arising from the pregnancy itself.[20]

The term "partial birth abortion" was defined by the statute as "an abortion procedure in which the person performing the abortion partially delivers vaginally a living unborn child before killing the unborn child and completing the delivery."[21] The term "partially delivers vaginally a living unborn child before killing the unborn child" was further defined as "deliberately and intentionally delivering into the vagina a living unborn child, or a substantial portion thereof, for the purpose of performing a procedure that the person performing such procedure knows will kill the unborn child and does kill the unborn child."[22]

Violation of the statute carried a prison term of up to twenty years and a fine of up to $25,000. In addition, a doctor who violated the statute was subject to the automatic revocation of his license to practice medicine in Nebraska.

Among his arguments, Dr. Carhart maintained that the meaning of the term "substantial portion" in the Nebraska statute was unclear and thus, could include the common D & E procedure in its ban of partial-birth abortions. Because the Nebraska legislature failed to provide a definition for "substantial portion," the U.S. Court of Appeals for the Eighth Circuit interpreted the Nebraska statute to proscribe both the D & X and D & E procedures: "if 'substantial portion' means an arm or a leg – and surely it must - then the ban ... encompasses both the D & E and the D & X procedures."[23] The Eighth Circuit acknowledged that during the D & E procedure, the physician often inserts his forceps into the uterus, grasps a part of the living fetus, and pulls that part of the fetus into the vagina. Because the arm or leg is the most common part to be retrieved, the physician would violate the statute.[24]

The state argued that the statute's scienter or knowledge requirement limited its scope and made it applicable only to the D & X procedure. According to the state, the statute applied only to the deliberate and intentional performance of a partia birth abortion; that is, the partial delivery of a living fetus vaginally, the killing of the fetus, and the completion of the delivery.[25] However, the Eighth Circuit found that the D & E procedure involves all of the same steps: "The physician intentionally brings a substantial part of the fetus into the vagina, dismembers the fetus, leading to fetal demise, and completes the delivery. A physician need not set out with the intent to perform a D & X procedure in order to violate the statute."[26]

The Supreme Court affirmed the Eighth Circuit's decision by a 5-4 margin. The Court based its decision on two determinations. First, the Court concluded that the Nebraska statute lacked any exception for the preservation of the health of the mother. Second, the Court found that the statute imposed an undue burden on the right to choose abortion because its language covered more than the D & X procedure.

Despite the Court's previous instructions in *Roe* and *Casey*, that abortion regulation must include an exception where it is "necessary, in appropriate medical judgment, for the preservation of the life or health of the mother," the state argued that Nebraska's partial-birth abortion statute did not require a health exception because safe alternatives remained available to women, and a ban on partial-birth abortions would create no risk to the health of women.[27] Although the Court conceded that the actual need for the D & X procedure was uncertain, it recognized that the procedure could be safer in certain circumstances.[28] Thus, the Court stated, "a statute that altogether forbids D & X creates a significant health risk . . . [t]he statute consequently must contain a health exception."[29]

In its discussion of the undue burden that would be imposed if the Nebraska statute was upheld, the Court maintained that the plain language of the statute covered both the D & X and D & E procedures.[30] Although the Nebraska State Attorney General offered an interpretation of the statute that differentiated between the two procedures, the Court was reluctant to recognize such a view. Because the Court traditionally follows lower federal court interpretations of state law and because the Attorney General's interpretative views would not bind state courts, the Court held that the statute's reference to the delivery of "a living unborn child, or a substantial portion thereof" implicated both the D & X and D & E procedures.[31]

Because the *Stenberg* Court was divided by only one member, Justice O'Connor's concurrence raised concern among those who support a woman's right to choose. Justice O'Connor's concurrence indicated that a state statute prohibiting partial-birth abortions would likely withstand a constitutional challenge if it included an exception for situations where the health of the mother is at issue, and if it was "narrowly tailored to proscribing the D & X procedure alone."[32] Justice O'Connor identified Kansas, Utah, and Montana as having partial-birth abortion statutes that differentiate appropriately between D & X and the other procedures.[33]

FEDERAL PROPOSALS TO BAN PARTIAL-BIRTH ABORTION

106th Congress

The Partial-Birth Abortion Ban Act of 1999, S. 1692, was introduced by then Senator Rick Santorum on October 5, 1999. The bill was approved by the Senate on October 21, 1999, by a vote of 63-34. H.R. 3660, the Partial-Birth Abortion Ban Act of 2000, was introduced by then Representative Charles T. Canady on February 15, 2000. H.R. 3660 was passed by the House on April 5, 2000, by a vote of 287-141. On May 25, 2000, the House passed S. 1692 without objection after striking its language and inserting the provisions of H.R. 3660. House conferees were subsequently appointed, but no further action was taken.

Both S. 1692 and H.R. 3660 would have imposed a fine and/or imprisonment not to exceed two years for any physician who knowingly performed a partial-birth abortion. Partial-birth abortion was defined as an abortion in which a person "deliberately and intentionally ... vaginally delivers some portion of an intact living fetus until the fetus is partially outside the body of the mother, for the purpose of performing an overt act that the person knows will kill the fetus" and actually performs the overt act that kills the fetus.[34] In addition to criminal penalties, S. 1692 and H.R. 3660 provided a private right of action for "[t]he father, if married to the mother at the time she receives a partial-birth abortion procedure, and if the mother has not attained the age of 18 years at the time of the abortion, the maternal grandparents of the fetus . . . unless the pregnancy resulted from the plaintiff's criminal conduct or the plaintiff consented to the abortion."[35]

When President Clinton vetoed a similar partial-birth abortion bill, H.R. 1122, during the 105th Congress, he focused on the bill's failure to include an exception to the ban that would permit partial-birth abortions to protect "the lives and health of the small group of women in tragic circumstances who need an abortion performed at a late stage of pregnancy to avert death or serious injury."[36] While S. 1692 and H.R. 3660 would have allowed a partial-birth abortion to be performed when it was necessary to save the life of the mother, such an abortion would not have been available when it was simply medically preferable to another procedure.

107th Congress

H.R. 4965, the Partial-Birth Abortion Ban Act of 2002, was introduced by Representative Steve Chabot on June 19, 2002. The bill was passed by the House on July 24, 2002, by a vote of 274-151. The measure was not considered by the Senate. H.R. 4965 would have prohibited physicians from performing a partial-birth abortion except when it was necessary to save the life of a mother whose life was endangered by a physical disorder, physical illness, or physical injury, including a lifeendangering physical condition caused by or arising from the pregnancy itself. The bill defined the term "partial-birth abortion" to mean an abortion in which "the person performing the abortion deliberately and intentionally vaginally delivers a living fetus until, in the case of a head-first presentation, the entire fetal head is outside the body of the mother, or, in the case of breech presentation, any part of the fetal trunk past the navel is outside the body of the mother for the purpose of performing an overt act that the person knows will kill the partially delivered living fetus."[37] Physicians who violated the act would have been subject to a fine, imprisonment for not more than two years, or both.

Although H.R. 4965 did not provide an exception for the performance of a partial-birth abortion when the health of the mother was at issue, supporters of the measure maintained that the bill was constitutional. They contended that congressional hearings and fact finding revealed that a partial-birth abortion is never necessary to preserve the health of a woman, and that such an abortion poses serious risks to a woman's health.

108th Congress

S. 3, the Partial-Birth Abortion Ban Act of 2003, was signed by the President on November 5, 2003 (P.L. 108-105). The House approved H.Rept. 108-288, the conference report for the measure, on October 2, 2003, by a vote of 281-142. The Senate agreed to the conference report on October 21, 2003, by a vote of 64-34.

In general, the act resembles the Partial-Birth Abortion Ban Act of 2002 in language and form. The act prohibits physicians from performing a partial-birth abortion except when it is necessary to save the life of a mother whose life is endangered by a physical disorder, physical illness, or physical injury, including a life-endangering physical condition caused by or arising from the pregnancy itself. Physicians who violate the act are subject to a fine, imprisonment for not more than two years, or both.

Although the Supreme Court previously held that restrictions on abortion must allow for the performance of an abortion when it is necessary to protect the health of the mother, the act does not include such an exception. In his introductory statement for the act, then Senator Rick Santorum discussed the act's lack of a health exception.[38] He maintained that an exception is not necessary because of the risks associated with partial-birth abortions. Senator Santorum insisted that congressional hearings and expert testimony demonstrate "that a partial birth abortion is never necessary to preserve the health of the mother, poses significant health risks to the woman, and is outside the standard of medical care."[39]

GONZALES V. CARHART

Within two days of the act's signing, federal courts in Nebraska, California, and New York blocked its enforcement.[40] On April 18, 2007, the Court upheld the Partial-Birth Abortion Ban Act of 2003, finding that, as a facial matter, it is not unconstitutionally vague and does not impose an undue burden on a woman's right to terminate her pregnancy.[41] In *Gonzales v. Carhart*, the Court distinguished the federal statute from the Nebraska law at issue in *Stenberg*.[42] According to the Court, the federal statute is not unconstitutionally vague because it provides doctors with a reasonable opportunity to know what conduct is prohibited.[43] Unlike the Nebraska law, which prohibited the delivery of a "substantial portion" of the fetus, the federal statute includes "anatomical landmarks" that identify when an abortion procedure will be subject to the act's prohibitions. The Court noted: "[I]f an abortion procedure does not involve the delivery of a living fetus to one of these 'anatomical landmarks'— where, depending on the presentation, either the fetal head or the fetal trunk past the navel is outside the body of the mother — the prohibitions of the act do not apply."[44]

The Court also maintained that the inclusion of a scienter or knowledge requirement in the federal statute alleviates any vagueness concerns. Because the act applies only when a doctor "deliberately and intentionally" delivers the fetus to an anatomical landmark, the Court concluded that a doctor performing the D & E procedure would not face criminal liability if a fetus is delivered beyond the prohibited points by mistake.[45] The Court observed: "The scienter requirements narrow the scope of the act's prohibition and limit prosecutorial discretion."[46]

In reaching its conclusion that the Partial-Birth Abortion Ban Act of 2003 does not impose an undue burden on a woman's right to terminate her pregnancy, the Court considered whether the federal statute is overbroad, prohibiting both the D & X and D & E procedures. The Court also considered the statute's lack of a health exception.

Relying on the plain language of the act, the Court determined that the federal statute could not be interpreted to encompass the D & E procedure. The Court maintained that the D & E procedure involves the removal of the fetus in pieces. In contrast, the federal statute uses the phrase "delivers a living fetus."[47] The Court stated: "D&E does not involve the delivery of a fetus because it requires the removal of fetal parts that are ripped from the fetus as they are pulled through the cervix."[48] The Court also identified the act's specific requirement of an "overt act" that kills the fetus as evidence of its inapplicability to the D & E procedure. The Court indicated: "This distinction matters because, unlike [D&X], standard D&E does not involve a delivery followed by a fatal act."[49] Because the act was found not to prohibit the D & E procedure, the Court concluded that it is not overbroad and does not impose an undue burden a woman's ability to terminate her pregnancy.

According to the Court, the absence of a health exception also did not result in an undue burden. Citing its decision in *Ayotte v. Planned Parenthood of Northern New England*,[50] the Court noted that a health exception would be required if it subjected women to significant health risks.[51] However, acknowledging medical disagreement about the act's requirements ever imposing significant health risks on women, the Court maintained that "the question becomes whether the act can stand when this medical uncertainty persists."[52] Reviewing its past decisions, the Court indicated that it has given state and federal legislatures wide discretion to pass legislation in areas where there is medical and scientific uncertainty.[53] The Court concluded that this medical uncertainty provides a sufficient basis to conclude in a facial challenge of the statute that it does not impose an undue burden.[54]

Although the Court upheld the Partial-Birth Abortion Ban Act of 2003 without a health exception, it acknowledged that there may be "discrete and well-defined instances" where the prohibited procedure "must be used."[55] However, the Court indicated that exceptions to the act should be considered in as-applied challenges brought by individual plaintiffs: "In an as-applied challenge the nature of the medical risk can be better quantified and balanced than in a facial attack."[56]

Justice Ginsburg authored the dissent in *Gonzales*. She was joined by Justices Stevens, Souter, and Breyer. Describing the Court's decision as "alarming," Justice Ginsburg questioned upholding the federal statute when the relevant procedure has been found to be appropriate in certain cases.[57] Citing expert testimony that had been introduced, Justice Ginsburg maintained that the prohibited procedure has safety advantages for women with certain medical conditions, including bleeding disorders and heart disease.[58]

Justice Ginsburg also criticized the Court's decision to uphold the statute without a health exception. Justice Ginsburg declared: "Not only does it defy the Court's longstanding precedent affirming the necessity of a health exception, with no carve-out for circumstances of medical uncertainty . . . it gives short shrift to the records before us, carefully canvassed by the District Courts."[59] Moreover, according to Justice Ginsburg, the refusal to invalidate the Partial-Birth Abortion Ban Act of 2003 on facial grounds was "perplexing" in light of the Court's decision in *Stenberg*.[60] Justice Ginsburg noted: "[I]n materially identical circumstances we held that a statute lacking a health exception was unconstitutional on its face."[61]

Finally, Justice Ginsburg contended that the Court's decision "cannot be understood as anything more than an effort to chip away at a right declared again and again by [the] Court — and with increasing comprehension of its centrality to women's lives."[62] Citing the language used by the Court, including the phrase "abortion doctor" to describe obstetrician-gynecologists and surgeons who perform abortions, Justice Ginsburg maintained that "[t]he Court's hostility to the right *Roe* and *Casey* secured is not concealed."[63] She argued that when a statute burdens constitutional rights and the measure is simply a vehicle for expressing hostility to those rights, the burden is undue.[64]

End Notes

[1] See Center for Reproductive Rights, *So-Called "Partial Birth Abortion" Bans,* at [http://www.crlp.org/st_law_pba.html] (last visited December 28, 2006).
[2] H.R. 1833, 104th Cong. (1995); H.R. 1122, 105th Cong. (1997).
[3] See Richmond Medical Center for Women v. Gilmore, 144 F.3d 326 (4th Cir. 1998) (Virginia Partial Birth Abortion Act is not unconstitutionally vague because it cannot "reasonably be read" to prohibit the D & E procedure); Hope Clinic v. Ryan, 195 F.3d 857 (7th Cir. 1999) (Illinois and Wisconsin statutes prohibiting partial-birth abortion are not unconstitutionally vague); Women's Medical Professional Corporation v. Voinovich, 130 F.3d 187 (6th Cir. 1997), *cert. denied,* 523 U.S. 1036 (1998) (Ohio statute banning partialbirth abortion imposes an undue burden on the ability to have an abortion because it restricts both the D & X and D & E procedures).
[4] 127 S. Ct. 1610 (2007).
[5] Roe v. Wade, 410 U.S. 113 (1973). *See also* CRS Report RL33467, *Abortion: Legislative Response,* by Jon O. Shimabukuro and Karen J. Lewis.
[6] *Roe,* 410 U.S. at 164-65.
[7] 505 U.S. 833 (1992).
[8] *See* Stenberg v. Carhart, 530 U.S. 914, 927 (2000).
[9] *Id.*
[10] *Id.*
[11] *See Hope Clinic,* 195 F.3d at 861.
[12] *See Voinovich,* 130 F.3d at 198.
[13] *Id.*
[14] *Hope Clinic,* 195 F.3d at 883.
[15] *Voinovich,* 130 F.3d at 199.
[16] *See* Grayned v. City of Rockford, 408 U.S. 104 (1972).
[17] *Id.*
[18] *Casey,* 505 U.S. at 877.
[19] 530 U.S. 914 (2000).
[20] Neb. Rev. Stat. § 28-328(1).
[21] Neb. Rev. Stat. § 28-326(9).
[22] *Id.*
[23] *Carhart,* 192 F.3d at 1150.
[24] *Id.*
[25] *Id.*
[26] *Id.*
[27] *Stenberg,* 530 U.S. at 931 (quoting *Roe,* 410 U.S. at 164-65).
[28] *Stenberg,* 530 U.S. at 937.
[29] *Id.* at 938.
[30] *Id.* at 939.

31 *Id.* at 940.
32 *Id.* at 950. *See also Stenberg*, 530 U.S. at 951 ("If there were adequate alternative methods for a woman safely to obtain an abortion before viability, it is unlikely that prohibiting the D & X procedure alone would 'amount in practical terms to a substantial obstacle to a woman seeking an abortion' [*citation omitted*] ... Thus, a ban on partial-birth abortion that only proscribed the D & X method of abortion and that included an exception to preserve the life and health of the mother would be constitutional in my view.").
33 *See Stenberg*, 530 U.S. at 950.
34 S. 1692, 106th Cong. (1999); H.R. 3660, 106th Cong. (2000).
35 *Id.*
36 Message to the House of Representatives Returning Without Approval Partial Birth Abortion Legislation, 33 Weekly Comp. Pres. Doc. 41 (October 13, 1997).
37 H.R. 4965, 107th Cong. § 3 (2002).
38 149 Cong. Rec. S2523 (daily ed. February 14, 2003) (statement of Sen. Santorum).
39 149 Cong. Rec., at S2523.
40 *Abortion Ban Blocked Again*, Wash. Post, November 7, 2003, at A2.
41 Unlike "as-applied" challenges, which consider the validity of a statute as applied to a particular plaintiff, facial challenges seek to invalidate a statute in all of its applications.
42 127 S. Ct. 1610 (2007).
43 *Id.* at 1628.
44 *Id.* at 1627.
45 *Id.* at 1628.
46 *Id.* at 1629.
47 18 U.S.C. § 1531(b)(1)(A).
48 *Gonzales*, 127 S. Ct. at 1630.
49 *Id.* at 1631.
50 546 U.S. 320 (2006)
51 *Gonzales*, 127 S.Ct. at 1635. For information on *Ayotte v. Planned Parenthood of Northern New England*, see CRS Report RL33467, *supra* note 5.
52 *Gonzales*, 127 S.Ct. at 1636.
53 *Id.*
54 *Id.* at 1637. The Court indicated that its conclusion was also supported by other considerations, including the availability of the D & E procedure.
55 *Id.* at 1638.
56 *Id.* at 1638-39.
57 *Id.* at 1641.
58 *Id.* at 1644-45.
59 *Id.* at 1646.
60 *Id.* at 1650.
61 *Id.*
62 *Id.* at 1653.
63 *Id.* at 1650.
64 *Id.* at 1653.

In: Abortion: Legislative and Legal Issues
Editor: Kevin G. Nolan

ISBN: 978-1-60741-522-0
© 2010 Nova Science Publishers, Inc.

Chapter 8

REQUIRING PARENTAL INVOLVEMENT IN A PREGNANT MINOR'S ABORTION DECISION: STATE LAWS AND RECENT DEVELOPMENTS[*]

Jon O. Shimabukuro and Tara Alexandra Rainso[2]

SUMMARY

State laws that require parental involvement in a pregnant minor's abortion decision have gained greater visibility in light of recent attempts by Congress to criminalize the interstate transport of a minor to obtain an abortion. At least forty-three states have enacted statutes that require a minor to seek either parental notification or parental consent before obtaining an abortion. This chapter discusses the validity of state parental involvement laws in the context of *Planned Parenthood of Southeastern Pennsylvania v. Casey, Ayotte v. Planned Parenthood of Northern New England*, and other U.S. Supreme Court cases that address a minor's right to choose whether to terminate her pregnancy. The report reviews the various state parental involvement law provisions, such as judicial bypass procedures and exceptions for medical emergencies. The report also highlights recent federal parental involvement legislation and provides a survey of current state parental involvement laws.

---

[*] This is an edited, reformatted and augmented version of a CRS Report for Congress publication, Report RL33625, dated January 9, 2007.

INTRODUCTION

State laws that require parental involvement in a pregnant minor's abortion decision have gained greater visibility in light of recent attempts by Congress to criminalize the interstate transport of a minor to obtain an abortion.[1] At least forty-three states have enacted statutes that require a minor to seek either parental notification or parental consent before obtaining an abortion. This chapter discusses the validity of state parental involvement laws in the context of *Planned Parenthood of Southeastern Pennsylvania v. Casey*, *Ayotte v. Planned Parenthood of Northern New England*, and other U.S. Supreme Court cases that address a minor's right to choose whether to terminate her pregnancy.

In *Casey,* the Court upheld the right of a woman to choose whether to terminate her pregnancy, but permitted certain restrictions on a minor's ability to obtain an abortion, such as state parental consent requirements.[2] In *Ayotte*, the Court reiterated that a state may require parental involvement in a pregnant minor's abortion decision.[3]

In addition to examining the relevant abortion decisions, this chapter reviews common state parental involvement law provisions, such as judicial bypass procedures and exceptions for medical emergencies. The report also highlights recent federal parental involvement legislation and provides a survey of current state parental involvement laws.

PLANNED PARENTHOOD OF SOUTHEASTERN PENNSYLVANIA V. CASEY AND AYOTTE V. PLANNED PARENTHOOD OF NORTHERN NEW ENGLAND

In *Roe v. Wade*, the U.S. Supreme Court held that a woman has a constitutional right to choose whether to terminate her pregnancy.[4] The Court in later cases has affirmed the basic right to an abortion, but also permitted restrictions on a woman's access to an abortion. *Casey* established that a state may require parental involvement in a pregnant minor's abortion decision if the involvement does not unduly burden the minor's right to choose whether to obtain an abortion. In that 1992 case, the Court considered a constitutional challenge to five provisions of the Pennsylvania Abortion Control Act of 1982. One provision required a pregnant minor seeking an abortion to obtain consent from one parent or guardian before the procedure.[5] The Court upheld the parental consent provision and also affirmed that a state law that banned abortion completely would be unconstitutional. In its holding, the Court shifted away from the trimester-based strict scrutiny standard of judicial review it used in *Roe* and articulated a new "undue burden" analysis. Courts will now invalidate a state-imposed abortion restriction if it imposes an "undue burden" on a woman's right to obtain an abortion.[6] Applying the new standard, the *Casey* Court held that the parental consent provision did not unduly burden a pregnant minor's right to obtain an abortion because it included exceptions in the event of a medical emergency and when the minor demonstrates to a court that parental consent is not in her best interests.[7]

In January 2006, the Court reiterated the validity of state laws that place certain restrictions on a pregnant minor's right to obtain an abortion. In *Ayotte*, the Court considered a constitutional challenge to a state statute requiring parental notification before a minor may obtain an abortion. The plaintiffs argued that the New Hampshire Parental Notification Prior to Abortion Act violates the right of a woman to obtain an abortion because it does not contain an exception to allow a pregnant minor to obtain an abortion without parental notification when the procedure is necessary to preserve the minor's health. In writing for an unanimous Court, Justice O'Connor stated explicitly that the holding did not revisit Court precedent regarding abortion.[8] Rather, the Court addressed the relatively narrow issue of remedies. It held that only certain applications of the act would violate a woman's constitutional right to an abortion, and remanded the case with orders for the lower courts to consider whether the act could be interpreted in a manner consistent with the judicial precedent that a state may not restrict access to an abortion when the health of the woman seeking the abortion is at issue.

Despite its narrow holding, the Court in *Ayotte* expressly affirmed two legal propositions relating to pregnant minors' access to abortions: states have the right to require parental involvement in a minor's abortion decision, and a state may not restrict access to an abortion that is necessary to protect the life or health of a woman seeking an abortion.[9]

PARENTAL NOTIFICATION AND PARENTAL CONSENT

Fourteen state parental involvement statutes require the consent of one parent before a pregnant minor may obtain an abortion, while twelve state statutes require only that the minor notify one or both parents that she intends to obtain an abortion. As discussed, the Court has held that a state law that requires parental involvement in a minor's abortion decision is unconstitutional if it unduly burdens the minor's right to terminate her pregnancy.

Several Court cases preceding *Casey* and *Ayotte* expressly established that a state parental involvement statute that permits a parent to unilaterally prohibit a minor from obtaining an abortion would be unconstitutional. In *Planned Parenthood of Central Missouri v. Danforth*, the Court held that a state parental involvement statute must provide an alternate procedure for a minor to obtain authorization for an abortion.[10] In *Belotti v. Baird*, the Court reiterated the *Danforth* holding and stated that such an alternative must provide a pregnant minor the opportunity to demonstrate that she is "mature enough and well enough informed" to make an abortion decision without parental involvement, or that the abortion is in her best interests.[11]

Judicial Bypass Procedure

Thirty-four state laws that require parental involvement in a pregnant minor's abortion decision provide for a judicial bypass procedure as the alternate means for a minor to obtain permission for an abortion. A judicial bypass procedure allows a minor who seeks an abortion to obtain permission from a court to waive the relevant parental involvement requirement. In cases preceding *Casey*, the Court held that adequate judicial bypass procedures are constitutional alternatives to state parental involvement statutes. Both *Danforth* and *Belotti,* for example, involved judicial bypass procedures that the Court upheld as valid safeguards of a pregnant minor's right to obtain an abortion.

While the Court has invalidated state parental *consent* laws that do not include judicial bypass procedures, it has not determined whether a state law that requires parental *notification* must contain a judicial bypass procedure. In *Ohio v. Akron Center for Reproductive Health, et al.*, the Court held that the Ohio parental notification statute at issue was constitutional, suggesting that the statute's judicial bypass procedure adequately protected a pregnant minor's right to obtain an abortion.[12] The Court expressly declined, however, to decide whether a state parental notification law that did not include a judicial bypass procedure would *per se* violate the Constitution. In *Lambert v. Wicklund*, the Court similarly declined to reach the question of whether a state parental notification law must contain a judicial bypass procedure.[13] Rather, the Court held narrowly that the Montana parental notification law at issue, which contained a judicial bypass procedure, did not place an undue burden on a pregnant minor's right to obtain an abortion.[14]

Although the Court has refused to address directly whether a state parental notification law must contain a judicial bypass procedure, Court precedent appears to suggest that a parental notification law would be unconstitutional if it did not provide a pregnant minor with some alternative to parental notification. In *H.L. v. Matheson*, the Court upheld as constitutional a state statute that requires an unemancipated minor who lives with her parents to notify them, "if possible," before she obtains an abortion, but includes exceptions for a minor who demonstrates that notification is not in her best interests.[15] Moreover, in *Belotti*, the Court indicated that a parental notification law would be unconstitutional if it did not provide an alternative to notification for a "mature" minor or when notification would not be in a minor's best interests.

The Court has declined to establish specific parameters for the adequacy of judicial bypass procedures in the context of state parental involvement laws. In writing for the majority in *Akron*, Justice Kennedy rejected the dissenting opinion's call to articulate specific procedural thresholds for the constitutionality of a judicial bypass alternative, such as whether it must be anonymous or only confidential, or how quickly a state must provide a pregnant minor with the opportunity for a court proceeding. He stated only that the Ohio judicial bypass procedure contained "reasonable steps" to protect the identity of pregnant minors seeking a judicial bypass and that the procedure included adequate provisions to expedite a pregnant minor's request for a proceeding.[16] The Court majority also held that a state may validly require a pregnant minor to establish "by clear and convincing evidence" during a judicial bypass hearing that she is mature enough to make an abortion decision without parental involvement.[17]

Medical Emergency Exception

State parental involvement statutes in Louisiana, Maryland, Massachusetts, and Ohio contain no express exception to protect the life or health of the pregnant minor. In *Ayotte*, the Court expressly reiterated its prior holdings in *Roe* and *Casey* that a state may not restrict access to an abortion that is necessary to preserve the life or health of the pregnant woman.[18] The Court also stated the factual proposition that in a small number of cases a pregnant minor requires an immediate abortion to prevent serious health consequences.[19] Therefore, a state statute that restricts a pregnant minor's access to an abortion likely must include an exception for medical emergencies involving the minor's health or life.

FEDERAL LEGISLATION IN THE 109TH CONGRESS

During the 109th Congress, legislation that would have prohibited the knowing transport of a minor across state lines with the intent to obtain an abortion was passed by both chambers. Senator John E. Ensign introduced S. 403, the Child Custody Protection Act, on February 16, 2005. The measure passed the Senate on July 25, 2006 by a vote of 65-34. Violators of the act would have been subject to a fine under title 18 of the U.S. Code, imprisonment for not more than one year, or both. The act included an exception for abortions that are necessary to save the life of the minor when endangered by a physical disorder, physical injury, or physical illness.

Representative Ileana Ros-Lehtinen introduced H.R. 748, the Child Interstate Abortion Notification Act, on February 10, 2005. The measure passed the House on April 27, 2005 by a vote of 270-157. The act would have also prohibited the interstate transport of a minor with the purpose of obtaining an abortion. In addition, H.R. 748 would have required a physician performing an abortion on a minor outside the minor's state of residence to notify her parents of the intended abortion at least 24 hours before the procedure. The act included exceptions to the notification provision for abortions necessary to save the minor's life.

On September 26, 2006, the House considered an amendment in the nature of a substitute to the version of S. 403 that was passed by the Senate. Voting 264-153, the House passed S. 403, now titled the Child Interstate Abortion Notification Act. Like H.R. 748, the House-passed version of S. 403 would have required a physician who performs or induces an abortion on a minor who is a resident of a state other than the state in which the abortion is performed to provide actual notice to a parent of the minor at least 24 hours before performing the abortion.

The House-passed version of S. 403 would have made additional changes not considered by H.R. 748, including a prohibition on the transportation of a minor across a state line and into a foreign nation in circumvention of a law requiring parental involvement in a minor's abortion decision; the denial of a civil action to a parent who has committed an act of incest with the minor; and the establishment of penalties for the transport of a minor across a state line for the purpose of obtaining an abortion by someone who has committed an act of incest with the minor.

Efforts to reconcile the differences in the Senate-passed version of S. 403 and the House-passed version of the measure were not successful.

The following table provides citations to state parental involvement statutes. Information concerning whether the applicable statute requires parental consent or notification is included in the table. Statutes that include judicial bypass provisions, medical emergency exceptions, and/or exceptions for a pregnant minor who is the victim of parental abuse or neglect are marked accordingly.

State Parental Involvement Statutes

State and Statute	Parental Involvement Required	Judicial Bypass Available	Medical emergency exception	Abuse/ Incest Exception
Alabama, § 26-21-1 *et seq.*	Consent; one parent	X	X	X
Alaska, §§ 18.16.020, 18.16.030	Not enforced: permanently enjoined by judicial order			
Arizona, § 36-2152	Consent; one parent	X	X	X
Arkansas, §§ 20-16-802(2), 20-16-804, 20-16-805(1), 20-16-808, 20-16-809	Consent; one parent	X	X	X
California Health & Safety Code, § 123450	Not enforced: permanently enjoined by judicial order			
Colorado, § 12.37.5.101 *et seq.*	Notification; one parent	X	X	X

(Continued)

State and Statute	Parental Involvement Required	Judicial Bypass Available	Medical emergency exception	Abuse/ Incest Exception
Delaware (applies to minors under 16), tit. 24 § 1780 *et seq.*	Notification; one parent (or adult relative)	X	X	
Florida, § 390.01114	Notification; one parent	X	X	X
Georgia, § 15-11-110 *et seq.*	Notification; one parent	X	X	
Idaho, § 18-609A	Consent; one parent (Not enforced: temporarily enjoined by judicial order)			
Illinois, ch. 750, § 70/1 *et seq.*	Notification; one parent (Not enforced: enjoined by judicial order)			
Indiana, § 16-34-2-4	Consent; one parent	X	X	
Iowa, § 135L.1 *et seq.*	Notification; one parent (or adult relative)	X	X	X
Kansas, § 65-6705	Notification; one parent	X	X	X
Kentucky, § 311.732	Consent; one parent	X	X	
Louisiana, §§ 40:1299.35.5 40:1299.35.7	Consent; one parent	X		X
Maryland Health-General Code, § 20-103	Notification; one parent	X		

(Continued)

State and Statute	Parental Involvement Required	Judicial Bypass Available	Medical emergency exception	Abuse/ Incest Exception
Massachusetts, ch. 112, § 12S	Consent; one parent	X		
Michigan, § 722.901 *et seq.*	Consent; one parent	X	X	
Minnesota, § 144.343 subd. 2	Notification; both parents	X	X	X
Mississippi, § 41-41-51 *et seq.*	Consent; both parents	X	X	
Missouri, § 188.028	Consent; one parent	X		
Montana, § 50-20-201 *et seq.*	Notification; one parent (Not enforced: enjoined by judicial order)			
Nebraska, § 71-6901 *et seq.*	Notification; one parent	X	X	X
Nevada, § 442.255 *et seq.*	Notification; one parent (Not enforced: enjoined by judicial order)			
New Hampshire, §§ 132:2b, 132:25	Notification; one parent (Not enforced: enjoined by judicial order)			
New Jersey, §§ 9:17A-1.1– 9:17A-1.12	Notification; one parent (Not enforced: enjoined by judicial order)			
New Mexico, § 30-5-1	Consent; one parent (Not enforced: enjoined by judicial order)			

(Continued)

State and Statute	Parental Involvement Required	Judicial Bypass Available	Medical emergency exception	Abuse/ Incest Exception
North Carolina, § 90-21.6 et seq.	Consent; one parent (or other adult relative)	X	X	
North Dakota, §§ 14-02.1-03, 14-02.1-03.1	Consent; both parents	X	X	
Ohio, §§ 2151.85, 2503.073, 2919.12, 2919.121	Consent; one parent	X	X	X
Oklahoma, § 1-740.1 et seq.	Notification; one parent	X	X	X
Pennsylvania, 18 § 5206 et seq.	Consent; one parent	X	X	
Rhode Island, §§ 23-4.7-4, 23-4.7-6	Consent; one parent	X	X	
South Carolina, § 44-41-30 – 44-41-36	Consent; one parent	X	X	X
South Dakota, §§ 34-23A-7, 34-23A-7.1	Notification; one parent	X	X	
Tennessee, § 37-10-301 et seq.	Consent; one parent	X	X	X
Texas, Fam Code § 33.002 et seq.	Consent; one parent	X	X	X
Utah, §§ 76-7-304, 76-7-305	Consent and notification; one parent	X (for consent Provision)	X (for Conesnt and Notification provisions)	X (for notification Provision)

(Continued)

State and Statute	Parental Involvement Required	Judicial Bypass Available	Medical emergency exception	Abuse/ Incest Exception
Virginia, § 16.1-241(V)	Consent; one parent (or other adult relative)	X	X	X
West Virginia, § 16-2F-1 *et seq.*	Notification; one parent	X	X	
Wisconsin, § 48.375	Consent; one parent (or other adult relative)	X	X	X
Wyoming, § 35-6-118	Consent; one parent	X	X	

End Notes

[1] *See* S. 403, 109th Cong. (2005); H.R. 748, 109th Cong. (2005).

[2] 505 U.S. 833 (1992).

[3] 126 S.Ct. 961 (2006).

[4] *Roe v. Wade*, 410 U.S. 113 (1973). For additional information on abortion, *see* CRS Report RL33467, *Abortion: Legislative Response*, by Karen J. Lewis and Jon O. Shimabukuro.

[5] The other provisions required spousal consent, a 24-hour waiting period, the pregnant woman's informed consent before she could obtain an abortion, and certain reporting for facilities that provide abortions. The plurality upheld the informed consent, waiting period, and reporting requirement provisions, finding that they did not impose undue burdens. It struck down the spousal consent provision, however, holding that it gave husbands too much control over their wives and could contribute to spousal abuse, thus imposing an undue burden on a woman's abortion decision.

[6] The plurality opinion defined "undue burden" as a "substantial obstacle in the path of a woman seeking an abortion of a nonviable fetus." *Casey*, 505 U.S. at 877. *Casey* was not the first judicial instance in which the Supreme Court held that a state cannot place a parental involvement restriction on a minor's right to obtain an abortion so that her parent or parents have absolute veto power over the decision. In *Planned Parenthood of Central Missouri v. Danforth*, 428 U.S. 52 (1976), the Court held that a state may not require the consent of parent or guardian of a pregnant minor seeking an abortion if such consent will unduly burden the minor's right to seek an abortion.

[7] *Casey*, 505 U.S. at 899.

[8] *Ayotte*, 126 S. Ct. at 965.

[9] *Ayotte*, 126 S. Ct. at 966-67.

[10] 428 U.S. 52 (1976). Minnesota, Mississippi, and North Dakota have laws that require the parental consent of both parents before a pregnant minor may obtain an abortion. The Court

has held that a state law that contains a two-parent consent provision is unconstitutional unless it contains an alternative for parental consent, such as a judicial bypass procedure.

[11] 443 U.S. 622, 642 (1979).

[12] 497 U.S. 502 (1990).

[13] 520 U.S. 292 (1997).

[14] *Id.* at 295.

[15] 450 U.S. 398 (1981).

[16] *Akron*, 497 U.S. at 513.

[17] *Akron*, 497 U.S. at 515.

[18] *Ayotte*, 126 S. Ct. at 967. In *Doe v. Bolton*, 410 U.S. 179 (1973), the Court held that, to determine whether an abortion is necessary to protect a woman's "health," a doctor may exercise his or her judgment based on various factors, such as a woman's physical, emotional, psychological, and familial well-being, as well as her age.

[19] *Ayotte*, 126 S. Ct. at 967.

INDEX

E

F

T